USAAF Antisubmarine Operations in World War Two

ALAN C. CAREY

Acknowledgements
The following individuals and organizations made this book possible: Key Publishing, Jerry Mason, Capt. USN (ret) of the U-boat Archives, Nickolas Veronico, the National Archives and Records Administration (NARA) at College Park, Maryland, and the Air Force Historical Research Agency (AFHRA) staff at Maxwell AFB, Alabama, including DAF Heraldry Air Force Historical Research Agency.

Published by Key Books
An imprint of Key Publishing Ltd
PO Box 100
Stamford
Lincs PE9 1XQ

www.keypublishing.com

The right of Alan C. Carey to be identified as the author of this book has been asserted in accordance with the Copyright, Designs and Patents Act 1988 Sections 77 and 78.

Copyright © Alan C. Carey, 2024

ISBN 978 1 80282 867 2

All rights reserved. Reproduction in whole or in part in any form whatsoever or by any means is strictly prohibited without the prior permission of the Publisher.

Typeset by SJmagic DESIGN SERVICES, India.

Contents

Introduction 4
Abbreviations 5
Chapter 1 Unprepared 6
Chapter 2 Creation of I Bomber Command 12
Chapter 3 Formation of First Antisubmarine Command 28
Chapter 4 Caribbean Operations (1942–43) 39
Chapter 5 The 480th Antisubmarine Group 48
Chapter 6 The 479th Antisubmarine Group 68
Chapter 7 Encounters with German Aircraft 78
Chapter 8 Conclusion 84
Appendix A U-boats Sunk by AAF Antisubmarine Squadrons 85
Appendix B Lineage of USAAF Antisubmarine Squadrons 87
Appendix C Squadron Information (July 1943) 88
Appendix D Bombardment Groups Assigned to Antisubmarine Command (July 1943) 89
Selected Bibliography 90
Endnotes 92
Index 94

Introduction

This work examines the history of antisubmarine warfare operations (ASW) conducted by the United States Army Air Force (USAAF) during World War Two, which played an underrated but essential role between 1942 and 1943. It begins with its unpreparedness to fight a war against the U-boat, to the establishment of the I Bomber Command, and the creation of the United States Army Air Force Antisubmarine Command.

USAAF antisubmarine squadrons sank 11 U-boats during operations conducted from bases in the Caribbean, the Eastern Seaboard of the United States, England, the Bay of Biscay, and the Mediterranean. Furthermore, the creation of the I Bomber Command and the First Antisubmarine Command is a story about the struggles between the branches of the armed forces to control antisubmarine operations and the squadrons assigned to engage the enemy.

At first, the USAAF was a piecemeal operation, with inadequate aircraft and untrained aircrews. However, it emerged as a proficient tactical fighting force with significant contributions, especially by the 479th and 480th Antisubmarine Groups based in England and French Morrocco.

Abbreviations

AAF	Army Air Force
AAFASC	Army Air Force Antisubmarine Command
ASWORG	Antisubmarine Operations Research Group
A/S	Antisubmarine/Antisubmarine squadron
ASW	Antisubmarine Warfare
BdU	German submarine headquarters
CARIBSEAFRON	Caribbean Sea Frontier
CINCLANT	Commander in Chief, Atlantic Fleet
COMINCH	Commander in Chief, United States Fleet
COMNAVNAW	Commander Naval Forces North African Waters
CNO	Chief of Naval Operations
EDC	Eastern Defense Command
MR	Medium-Range aircraft
NANCF	North Atlantic Naval Coastal Frontier
SADU	Sea Search Attack Development Unit
USAAF	United States Army Air Force
LR	Long-range aircraft
VLR	Very Long-Range aircraft

Chapter 1
Unprepared

The U-boat War in World War Two, like that of World War One, was a struggle for mastery over the sea lanes. Germany's strategy was to block the flow of war materials and other essential goods from North America to the United Kingdom. The mastermind behind the German U-boat war was Admiral Karl Dönitz, Commander-in-Chief of U-boats and later Commander-in-Chief of the German Navy. He planned to conduct an all-out campaign to sink the maximum number of ship tonnage per submarine. Yet, at the outset, due to his Navy's size and logistics, he was limited in what his fleet could accomplish.

During the first seven months of the war, U-boat operations were conducted against shipping off the west and north-western approaches of Great Britain, the English Channel, the North Sea, waters off Norway and Sweden, and the Bay of Biscay. Establishing U-boat bases in France, located along the Bay of Biscay, extended operations eastward to North American waters. Establishing those bases in France with increased submarine production allowed Dönitz to launch his strategy, in which groups of U-boats, between eight and 20, fanned out across the Atlantic in search of merchant shipping. The first U-boat to make an initial contact would radio the convoy's course, speed, and location to German submarine headquarters (BdU) at Lorient, France, and the rest of the pack would group on receipt of the message and intercept the ship.

The German U-boat juggernaut continued throughout most of 1942, with the USAAF and US Navy (USN) on the defensive since the two services lacked suitable aircraft and trained personnel, effectively allowing Germany to operate with impunity along the eastern shores of the United States.

Pre-war plans drawn up by the Army and USN called for the United States Army Air Corps (USAAC), the predecessor of the Army Air Force, to support the country's naval forces in case enemy activity endangered the Eastern Seaboard of the United States. The Navy's air arm in 1941–42 lacked aircraft

Above left: Konteradmiral (rear admiral) and later Großadmiral (Grand Admiral) Karl Dönitz commanded Germany's U-boat fleet and desired to strangle the shipping lifeline between North America and the United Kingdom. (Courtesy of the National Archives and Records Administration, hereafter referred to as NARA)

Above right: A convoy of 24 merchant ships is seen steaming south of Newfoundland on July 28, 1942. (Courtesy of NARA 80-G-21187)

General Henry "Hap" Arnold, commanding general of the Army Air Force, viewed antisubmarine warfare (ASW) as an offensive mission to defeat the U-boat menace. (National Museum of the Air Force, 021002-O-9999G-013)

capable of long-range (LR) operations of 400–600 miles or very long-range patrols over the ocean (with a radius of up to 1,000 miles). To supplement its meager antisubmarine forces, the US Navy requested the AAF, commanded by General Henry "Hap" Arnold, to provide suitable aircraft and crews. The Navy emphasized that naval aircraft would conduct overwater operations close to the eastern seaboard to protect merchant shipping sailing close to shore. However, the AAF emphasized an offensive doctrine of locating and attacking enemy submarines hundreds of miles out at sea before U-boats could conduct operations off the North American Coast. At the same time, the Navy held a defensive position to protect ships sailing along coastal waters. Hence, the two military forces had divergent viewpoints on conducting the U-boat war. That disagreement would last throughout the Army's role in antisubmarine warfare.

Operation Drumbeat

The sudden entry of the United States into World War Two on December 7, 1941, caught Admiral Dönitz by surprise, since he had no submarines immediately available to send to North American waters. He did allocate five long-distance submarines–all he could quickly make ready–to Operation *Drumbeat*, his code name for operations against shipping in US coastal sea lanes. After sailing from France, those submarines took about three weeks to reach American waters. Modified to carry an extra 20 tons of fuel, they could remain on patrol for two to three weeks and averaged 41 days at sea. Admiral Dönitz extended this time by refueling and resupplying operational submarines from specially modified ones he named "milch cows." These carried enough fuel and supplies to resupply U-boats and extend their time at sea to an average of 62 days with one refueling and 81 days with a second refueling.

The presence of U-boats off North America began on December 31, 1941, when a Coast Guard cutter reported a periscope in Portland, Maine. That incident was followed on January 7, 1942, when an Army plane sighted a submarine off the coast of New Jersey. On that day, the Navy reported the presence of a fleet of U-boats in the waters south of Newfoundland. U-*66,* U-*109,* U-*123,* U-*125,* and U-*130* arrived off the Eastern Seaboard of the United States on January 13, 1942, to begin conducting the U-boat campaign called Operation *Paukenschlag* (*Drumbeat*), planned by Admiral Dönitz to substantially reduce Allied shipping and score a propaganda coup by conducting submarine operations with relative immunity in sight of the United States' mainland.

Those submarines left Lorient, France, between December 23 and 27, 1941, and stationed some 60 miles off Montauk Point, Long Island. Torpedoes from the Type IXB U-boat U-*123*, commanded by Korvettenkapitän Reinhard Hardegen, struck the Panamanian tanker *Norness,* which was carrying 12,000 tons of fuel, almost twice the fueling capacity of the USS *Enterprise* (CV-6). U-*123* proceeded to sink five other ships, two off New York and three off North Carolina. Hardegen ran out of torpedoes and began the trek home only to encounter additional merchant ships on January 25 and 27; the U-boat's deck gun finished off three ships, bringing the U-boat's total to nine ships sunk, totaling 53,000 tons. Total Allied losses for January and February 1942 in the North Atlantic were 65 ships, or 389,218 tons.[1]

 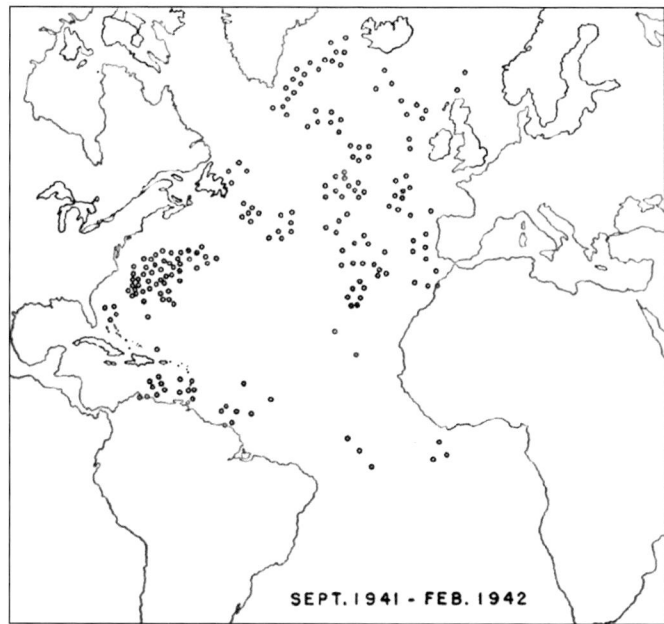

Above left: Korvettenkapitän Reinhard Hardegen, shown here, commanded U-*123* during the first Operation *Drumbeat* off North America. (Author's collection/unknown source)

Above right: Locations of ships sunk by German U-boats between September 1941 and February 1942. (Air Force Historical Research Agency (AFHRA Reel A4058, 90)

By February 1942, German submarines had moved further south to Florida, the Gulf of Mexico, and the Caribbean. The AAF and Navy were caught unprepared for submarine warfare before the US officially entered the war. However, between September 1939 and December 1941, American aircraft and naval surface units protected mainly British shipping by providing neutrality patrols. However, it would take nearly two years for the Navy and Army to implement a well-organized plan to conduct adequate antisubmarine warfare once U-boats began operating off North America.

Admiral Ernest King, Commander in Chief, Atlantic Fleet (CINCLANT), later promoted to Chief of Naval Operations (CNO), became the first commanding officer to plan antisubmarine operations by first implementing an organized set of procedures named command and control measures for ASW with one of the earliest being the establishment of individual sea frontiers beginning on July 1, 1941. Those frontiers extended outward from North America into the Atlantic, the Caribbean, and South America. The primary duty of each frontier command was to defend shipping by providing air coverage for transatlantic convoys and conducting antisubmarine warfare (ASW) operations within its zone of responsibility. All military forces in each frontier fell under the complete operational control of the respective Commander Sea Frontier.

The Navy established five frontiers: the Eastern Sea Frontier, the Canadian Coastal Zone, the Gulf Sea Frontier, the Panama Sea Frontier, and the Caribbean Sea Frontier. Additionally, the vastness of the Atlantic required the establishment of zones around Bermuda, the Azores, Brazil, the Southwest Atlantic, and the Southeast Atlantic. The Eastern Sea Frontier extended from the Canadian border to northern Florida. The Gulf Sea Frontier encompassed the Gulf of Mexico as far south as the border between Mexico and Guatemala, most of the Florida Coast, the Bahamas' northern half, and Cuba's eastern half. The Panama Sea Frontier covered Central America and Colombia's Pacific and Atlantic coasts, and the Caribbean Sea Frontier included the rest of the Caribbean and the north-east coast of

Above left: Following President Roosevelt's decision to have one officer serve as wartime Chief of Naval Operations (CNO) and Commander in Chief of the US Fleet, Admiral Stark, seen here, was relieved by Admiral King as Chief of Naval Operations. (Naval History and Heritage Command, NH 49967)

Above right: Admiral Ernest J. King, seen here, viewed antisubmarine operations as defensive, protecting coastal merchant ships sailing off the US's eastern seaboard. (Naval History and Heritage Command 80-G-302273)

South America. The US Navy sent out every available aircraft and blimp to hunt U-boats along the East Coast, with the Army Air Force contributing but under the operational control of the Navy. The North Atlantic Naval Coastal Frontier Commander, later the Eastern Sea Frontier, was initially responsible for engaging in antisubmarine operations but with only 20 surface vessels at his disposal.[2]

American antisubmarine efforts began months before the United States entered the war when the US Army Air Corps later named the Army Air Force, sent two squadrons to Newfoundland to participate in neutrality patrols. In May 1941, the 21st Reconnaissance Squadron began operating from Newfoundland Airport, operating B-17s and B-18s. There, it patrolled in cooperation with the Royal Canadian Navy and Air Force but sighted no German submarines before rotating back to the US in September. The 21st was relieved by the 41st Reconnaissance Squadron (Heavy), which acted as a separate unit of the Army Air Force, under administrative control of the First Air Force but served under command and control of the Canadian and British Newfoundland Base Command. To avoid the problems over command and control of Army air units, the squadron received verbal orders from the Canadians or British. It could patrol any area and attack submarines at the discretion of the squadron commander, a direct line of communication. On October 26, 1941, one 41st Squadron plane unsuccessfully attacked a U-boat, the first offensive engagement by the Air Force.

During the war, the Allies fought against several types of U-boats; the IXC and VII were the main types that Army antisubmarine squadrons encountered. Meanwhile, US Army aircraft assigned to spot and engage hostile submarines were the Douglas B-18 Bolo, Lockheed A-20 Havoc, the Lockheed

A-29 Hudson, B-17 Flying Fortress, the Consolidated B-24 Liberator, the North American B-25 Mitchell, and the Lockheed B-34 Lexington. Most aircraft deployed for such work during the first months of the war lacked radar and trained personnel to fight an effective battle, and there was no specific training program to conduct such work.

A map showing the Sea Frontiers and sectors covered by Army and Naval air and surface assets as of August 1, 1942. (AFHRA, Reel A4070, 349)

Above left: The Type VIIC U-boat, considered the workhorse of the German submarine force, was a 220ft (67m), 769-ton vessel with a top surface speed of 17.7 knots, submerged at 7.7 knots, with a diving depth of 721ft (220m). Offensively, the VIIC carried a maximum load of 14 torpedoes, fired through four tubes forward and two aft. (Courtesy of NARA via Tom Gates)

Above right: The Type IXC was nearly 400 tons heavier and 30ft longer than the VIIC. It could carry 22 torpedoes fired from four tubes forward and two aft. The offensive weaponry comprised 88 and 105 deck guns to sink unarmed merchant shipping effectively. Defensive weapons ranged from a 12.7mm machine gun to a 40mm cannon. (Courtesy of NARA via Tom Gates)

Right: The comparative size of American antisubmarine aircraft and the Type VIIC German U-boat. (Source: A. Timothy Warnock, *Air Power versus U-boats, Confronting Hitler's Submarine Menace in the European Theater.* Air Force History and Museum. (The US Army Air Forces in World War II Air Force History and Museum Program (1999), 3, © in the public domain)

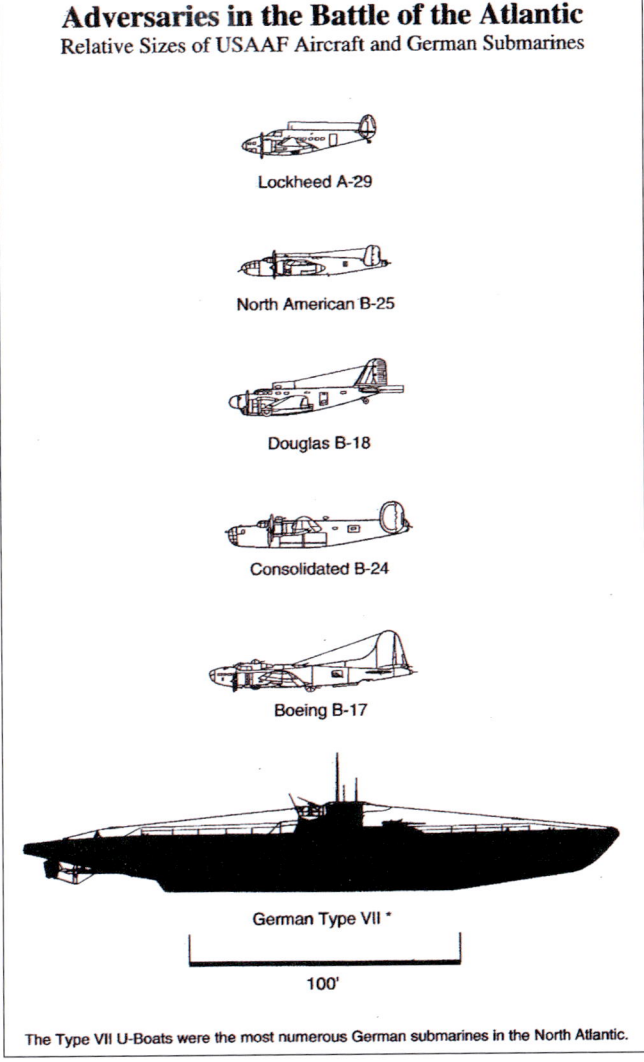

Adversaries in the Battle of the Atlantic
Relative Sizes of USAAF Aircraft and German Submarines

Lockheed A-29
North American B-25
Douglas B-18
Consolidated B-24
Boeing B-17
German Type VII
100'

The Type VII U-Boats were the most numerous German submarines in the North Atlantic.

Chapter 2
Creation of I Bomber Command

On September 5, 1941, the USAAF activated the 1st Bomber Command, First Air Force, with the primary duty of conducting antisubmarine operations along the east coast of the United States, where German U-boats were operating. The I Bomber Command operated under the control of the First Air Force from September 5, 1941, to October 15, 1942. On December 8, 1941, aircraft of that command began over-water reconnaissance patrols, providing convoy coverage and to conduct antisubmarine warfare.

In January 1942, the command began cooperating with the Navy on antisubmarine patrol and operations. The AAF established The Gulf Task Force, I Bomber Command at the end of May 1942, when the Army added the Gulf of Mexico region to the antisubmarine units of the First Air Force. Available Army Air Corps units for antisubmarine operations along the Eastern Sea Frontier in early 1942 consisted of the following:

Langley Field, VA
2nd Bombardment Group (Heavy)
22nd Bombardment Group (Heavy)
18th Reconnaissance Squadron (Medium)
Bangor, Maine
43rd Bombardment Group (Heavy)
13th Bombardment Squadron (Heavy)
Westover Field, Mass
34th Bombardment Group (Heavy)
1st Reconnaissance Squadron (Heavy)

Source: Air Force Historical Research Agency (AFHRA) at Maxwell AFB, Alabama, Reel A4058, 131.

The Army command bore the brunt of the U-boat war for nearly ten months. During daylight hours, the Army Air Support Command operated patrols in single-engine land observation planes extending about 40 miles offshore off Portland, Maine, to Wilmington, N.C. Those planes were not armed and carried only sufficient fuel for flights lasting between two and three hours, and pilots were inexperienced in the type of work. At any one time, no more than ten observation planes, some operated by the Civil Air Patrol (CAP), were in the air along the Eastern Coastal Frontier.

I Bomber Command's first logo has a blue disc edged in gold with a gold bomb. The command became responsible for forming Army Air Force (AAF) antisubmarine operations. (Air Force Combat Units of World War II, USAF Heraldry Division

Vice Admiral Adolphus Andrews, USN, Commander, Eastern Sea Frontier. (Naval History and Heritage Command, NH 56042)

COMINCH rebuffed repeated requests for additional naval vessels and aircraft for ASW, and argued that such assets were needed in the Pacific; thus, the burden fell to the limited resources available along the Eastern Seaboard. Admiral Adolphus Andrews, Commander, Eastern Sea Frontier, summed up the situation on January 14, 1942, in a cablegram to COMINCH in which he stated that there were no effective planes attached to the frontier, First, Third, Fourth, or Fifth District capable of maintaining long-range seaward patrols. In December 1941, the naval planes at the disposal of Admiral Andrews totaled 103. However, most were trainers or utility planes. Andrews spoke of the situation:

> The Army Air Support Command operates during daylight hours patrols in single-motored land-observation planes extending about 40 miles offshore from Portland, Maine, to Wilmington, N. C. The pilots are inexperienced in the type of work they are endeavoring to do. Not more than ten of these observation planes are in the air along the Coastal Frontier at any one time.[1]

A month later, the Navy reported 63 aircraft, including four airships, were available for duty between Salem, Massachusetts, and Elisabeth, New Jersey. Of those, 49 were in commission, and the majority could carry only one depth bomb or depth charge. The Commander of the North Atlantic Naval Coastal Frontier (NANCF) reported to COMINCH on January 14, 1942, requesting one squadron of patrol planes. However, COMINCH said additional allocations of such aircraft would depend on future production. Therefore, the absence of a significant naval air force with adequate aircraft caused the Army Air Force to carry the burden of antisubmarine patrolling.

The Air Force's First Support Command reported 114 planes on hand, 93 in commission, but most were observation planes; the I Bomber Command numbered 119 planes, of which only 46 were in commission. By the end of January, the command had approximately 100 twin-engine aircraft capable of carrying a bomb load, all medium-range aircraft such as the B-18 and B-25. It would be months before the long-range B-24 would reach antisubmarine units in sizable numbers. The command began to grasp the situation by the middle of March 1942. Yet, ASW is a specialized duty, and the command still lacked organization, crews trained in the strategies and tactics of conducting such work, and aircraft fitted with submarine detection equipment. By early 1942, the command grew in strength, having the 2nd, 13th, and 45th Bombardment Groups and two reconnaissance squadrons, the 3rd and 92nd, available for antisubmarine duty, and by the end of March 1942, AAF planes doubled their operational hours when compared to those flown in January.

The Navy's inventory of aircraft available for antisubmarine operations also lacked sufficient numbers, especially medium-range aircraft. The Army could muster 46 medium-range bombers for duty along the east coast while the Navy could muster 19 of the 46 planes in commission along the coast; many of them were the OS2U Kingfisher observation planes capable of carrying only two depth bombs. Additionally, as of January 31, 1942, the Navy lacked sufficient long-range (LR) planes, capable of traveling 600 miles or more out to sea with a full bomb load.[2]

By the end of March, there was a noticeable improvement in the number of Army aircraft and Naval surface vessels available. Nonetheless, U-boats continued to move towards US coastal waters in

Above left: The A-20A Havoc medium bomber was the model used by early United States Army Air Force (USAAF) antisubmarine squadrons along with the B-18 and A-29. General performance with a crew of three was a maximum speed of 317mph (510km/h), a surface ceiling of 23,700ft (7,200m), a range of 945 miles (1,521km), a maximum bomb load of 4,000lb (1,800kg), and armed initially, with .30 side-mounted fuselage blisters and one .30 in the ventral position, and some were equipped with Air-to-Surface Vessel (ASV) radar. Later models were equipped with up to eight .50 machine guns. Its overall length was nearly 48ft (14.6m) with a wing span of 61ft (18.6m). (AFHRA, Reel A4088, 867)

Above right: The B-17E and F were the primary variants of the B-17 Flying Fortress used by the USAAF for antisubmarine duty. They had a top speed of approximately 287mph (462km/h). They had an overall length of 74ft (22.5m) with a wingspan of 103ft (931m). The armament comprised eight .50 caliber (12.7mm) machine guns. The SCR-517 or the SCR-717 radar replaced the ball turret, thus reducing the number of gun positions. The maximum bomb and depth bomb load on long-range missions was 4,500lb or 2,000kg. (AFHRA, Reel A4088, 876)

The Douglas B-18 Bolo was the first Army aircraft utilized in large numbers to fight the crisis. The aircraft's general specifications included a crew of six with a top speed of 216mph (238km/h), a range of 900mi (1,400km), a service ceiling of 23,900ft (7,300m), a bomb load of 2,000lb (910kg), and armed with three 30-caliber (7.62). Its overall length was nearly 58ft (14.6m), with a wing span of 89ft (27m). The aircraft usually carried the Mk II radar, as did the A-29 Hudson. (Author's collection)

increasing numbers, taking a higher toll on merchant shipping. In response, as increasing numbers of Allied naval vessels and aircraft became available, U-boats found themselves forced to submerge, preventing the free hunting they had enjoyed during the previous two months. Meanwhile, a handful of Army medium-range planes were sent to Greenland and Iceland. At the same time, the 20th Bombardment Squadron began operating B-17s out of Newfoundland.

On May 15, 1942, the I Bomber Command aircraft extended convoy coverage from Key West, Florida, to the Chesapeake Bay, extending to the Caribbean in the summer to protect oil and bauxite shipping.

A more detailed picture of the status of Army antisubmarine warfare strength on January 31, 1942, is presented below and shows that of the 46 available aircraft, 37 percent were in commission to perform anti-submarine warfare:

Location	Type	Total	In Commission	Out of Commission
Grenier, NH	A-20A	1	0	1
Westover, Mass	B-18	1	0	1
Mitchell Field, NY	B-18M	3	2	1
Langley Field, VA	DB-7B	*55	0	55
Westover	B-25	1	0	1
	B-25A	2	2	0
	B-25B	19	14	5
Mitchell	B-18A	2	2	0
	B-25	2	0	2
	B-25A	1	0	1
	B-25B	8	7	1
Langley	B-17	9	8	1
	B-17E	2	1	1
	B-18A	3	2	1
	B-25	1	0	1
	B-25A	9	8	1
Total		119	46	73

* The DB-7 was an export version of the Douglas A-20 Havoc.
Source: Air Force Historical Research Agency (AFHRA) at Maxwell AFB, Alabama, Reel A4058, 185.

I Bomber Command relied on the B-18 and B-25 bombers to fly up to 300 miles offshore and its heavy B-17 bomber to cover 600 miles over the Atlantic. Until March 1942, the command had only three aircraft flying daily from Westover Field, Massachusetts, and three from Mitchell Field, New York, which was insufficient to cover the entire Eastern Sea Frontier. Yet, most aircraft carried demolition bombs instead of depth charges; they could not fly at night, and only four aircraft were equipped with radar.

The B-24D USAAF antisubmarine model Liberator usually carried a crew of ten. Its general characteristics included the SCR-517 and SCR-717 radar installed in the bottom tunnel or ball turret position, a top speed of 297mph (478km/h), a surface ceiling of 1,540mi (2,480km), a very long range (VLR) of 1,200mi (1,900km), a maximum bomb load of 2,700lb (1,200kg) and armed with one tail turret with two .50 machine guns, one top turret with two .50 machine guns, one 1 x 2 waist gun in each of the waist hatches, and two hand-held .50 nose guns. A hydraulically-driven nose turret was installed on later variants. Its overall length was 67ft with a wingspan of 110ft. (AFHRA, Reel 4088, 849, and 857)

Command and Control

American intelligence capability was weak during 1942, with the Navy failing to provide information to the AAF received from the British. Even if intelligence filtered down to other commands, it lost usefulness because the Navy did not quickly communicate information to Army organizations. It was not until 1943 that American intelligence could pinpoint the exact location of hostile submarines after the British shared Enigma's code-breaking machine, which could decipher German military codes. By August 1943, the Americans and British were reading German messages as soon as the radio operator sent them. Still, in 1942, there was no such capability. The US Army and Navy were operating in near chaos, trying to grasp and undertake the war against the U-boat as the two jockeyed to take control of the mission. The jurisdiction of whether the Army or Navy should command air activities for antisubmarine operations was highly contentious between the two services. Generally speaking, the Army argued that land-based aircraft should be its responsibility, whether patrolling over land or water.

In contrast, the Navy argued that convoy patrol and seaborne targets would be the Navy's responsibility. It depended on the service's primary obligation in which the Army claimed land-based aircraft engaged in antisubmarine warfare operations gave it precedence and in which naval land-based air units would fall under Army command. There was no argument over the Navy's control over seaward aviation, seaplanes, and carrier-based aircraft, as they fell under the Navy's control. The Army protested such a concept. The Navy assumed responsibility for offshore operations, leaving the Army with a supporting role. Therefore, I Bomber Command and I Air Support Command would operate seaward patrol missions whenever the naval authority requested it.

However, Army officials argued that jurisdiction should fall under its command as its service was vital to antisubmarine operations. General Arnold proposed to settle the argument in a letter to Admiral King dated May 9, 1942. He recommended establishing a Coastal Command within the Army Air Corps, which would have operations similar to the Royal Air Force (RAF) operating "when necessary, under the proper control of the Navy." By May 1942, the two services found it imperative to resolve the question over jurisdiction as sinkings of Allied shipping reached a critical point as U-boats moved south to Florida, the Gulf of Mexico, and the Caribbean. General Arnold held, "The submarine is a terrible menace and must be a target for our bombers. Their destruction is one of our primary problems. I am convinced, therefore, that we must hit them first."[3]

Lt. General Joseph T. NcNarney would develop a plan for land-based AAF antisubmarine warfare under which the AAF organized the Army Air Forces Antisubmarine Command. (US Air Force).

Once the submarine menace appeared, it became clear that long- and medium-range land-based bombers would to the Army and Navy be an indispensable part of the antisubmarine campaign. The Navy had so few and requested such aircraft from Army production runs. The request did nothing to improve relations between the services as the various Army commands viewed it as a means for the Navy to build a strategic bombing force. The Navy's request for Army bombers again raised the question of jurisdiction and organization. General Arnold argued that making such a naval force would lead to duplication of operations and deny the essential differences between armies and navies.

Hereto, command boundaries overlapped between the Army and Navy as the First Air Force and I Bomber Command extended operations far beyond the Eastern Sea Frontier and into the Gulf of

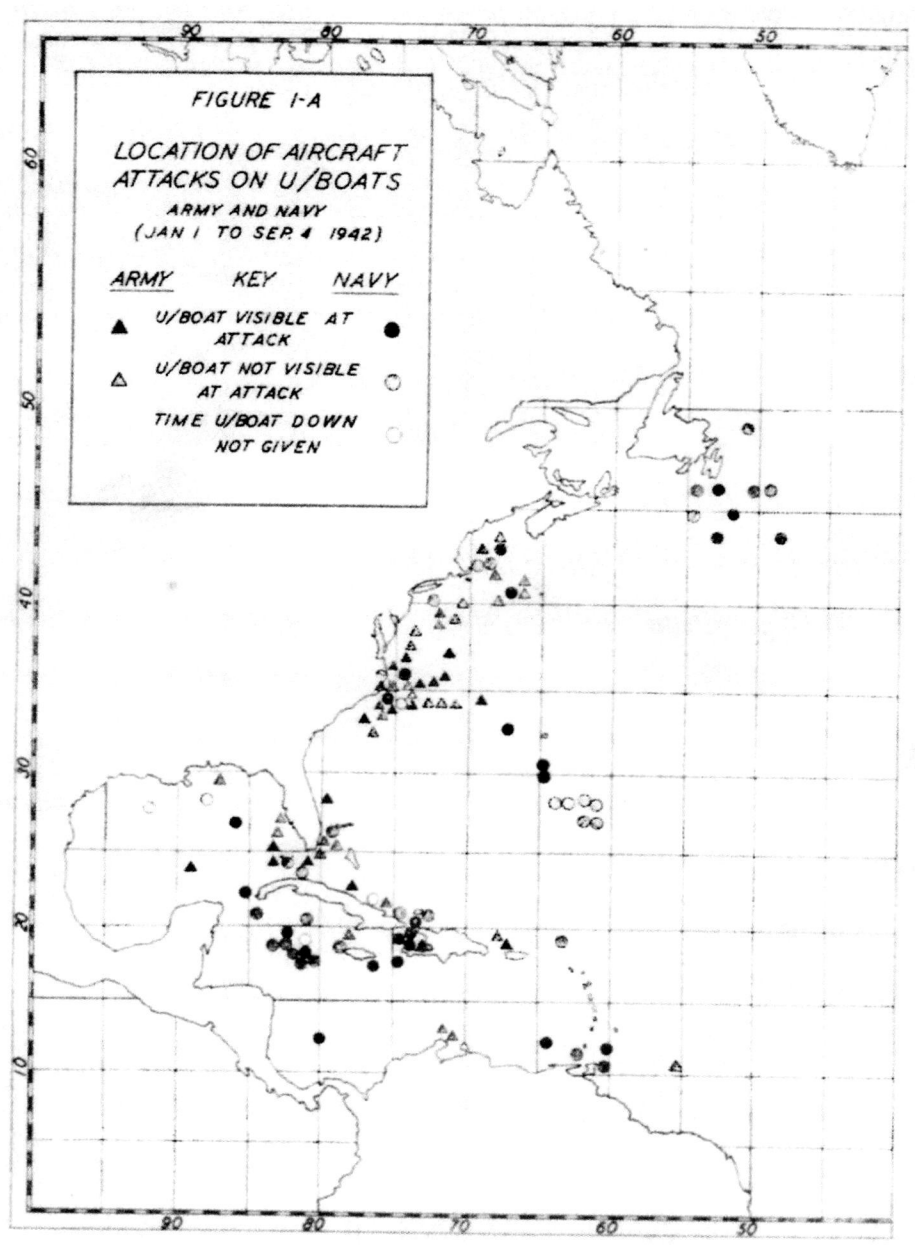

A map detailing AAF and Navy encounters against German U-boats between January and September 1942. (AFHRA Reel 4058, 113)

Mexico (Gulf Sea Frontier). However, the Army could handle antisubmarine operations when sufficient numbers of aircraft and trained flight crews were available. The Navy was not ready to undertake such an operation at the time. General Joseph T. McNarney of the War Department Reorganization Board described the joint command situation in April 1942, "At present, the Bomber Command is allocated to the Eastern Sea Frontier for operational control… The Air Support Command is under the Bomber

Command for operational control. The Bomber Command is operating under a directive from the Navy, a two-page, seven-paragraph letter."[4]

While the Navy and Army attempted to find a solution or compromise on the unity of command and jurisdiction, a second Army Air Force unit was organized for the ASW in June 1942. Based at Langley Field, Virginia, the Sea Search-Attack Development Unit (SADU) undertook a combined mission to develop tactics and techniques for acquiring antisubmarine devices and conducting general research. Meanwhile, Army aircraft lacked air-to-surface radar and began equipping planes with the SCR-520 and -521, which, in turn, were replaced by the SCR-517 with the "C" type being the smallest and lightest in weight and installed on the B-17, B-18, and B-24, B-25 and B-34. A skilled radar operator using the device could identify a surfaced submarine at approximately 40 miles and a conning tower at 15–30 miles. The number of available aircraft fitted with radar fluctuated during 1942, corresponding to the number of available operational aircraft.

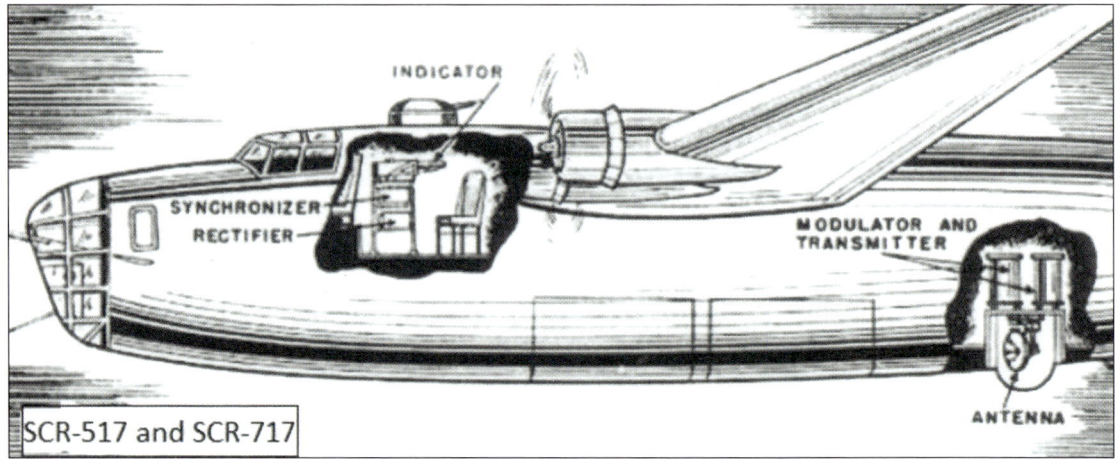

The main air-to-surface radar sets for antisubmarine tracking were the SCR-517 series and SCR-717, which are shown here on a Consolidated B-24D Liberator. The -517's maximum reliable range for surfaced submarines was 18 miles, while the -717's maximum range for spotting submarines was up to 20 miles. (Source: Joint Committee on New Weapons and Equipment. *US Radar Operational Characteristics of Radar Classified by Tactical Application*, FTP-217: 72)

The radar pod, shown here, on a B-17 Flying Fortress, housed the modulator, transmitter, and antennae. (AFHRA Reel A04088, 864)

Tactical Number of Army Aircraft Fitted with Radar in 1942

Date	A20	A-29	B-17	B-18	B-24	B-25	B-34	No. Fitted with Radar
January 1942	55	–	11	13	–	13	–	0
February	55	17	12	9	–	26	–	0
March	50	16	11	23	–	29	–	4
April	50	11	5	23	–	31	–	16
May	47	16	15	22	–	33	–	33
June	45	25	14	26	–	40	–	22
July	32	23	12	41	–	50	56	50
August	31	22	12	30	–	52	48	40
September	28	20	13	22	2	41	40	34
October	22	19	12	14	3	35	43	27
November	5	22	11	18	3	33	47	31
December	1	22	12	24	29	42	43	63

Source: Air Force Historical Research Agency (AFHRA) Reel A4058, 1062).

Using B-18s and B-24s, SADU trained combat crews in the tactical employment of radar and additional equipment while establishing guidelines for antisubmarine patrolling. This consisted of routine patrols where submarines might exist, air escorting convoys within range of land-based aircraft, and intensive patrols craft and providing intensive patrol of an area where an enemy submarine was spotted.

By April 1942, I Bomber Command operated under the Eastern Sea Frontier and the Gulf Sea Frontier, which the Navy commanded; therefore, AAF units could be connected administratively or operationally with two defense commands, two sea frontiers, two Air Forces (the First and Third,) and an antisubmarine bomber command. However, the Army argued that unity of command was essential to becoming an effective fighting force. On May 20, 1942, Major General Eisenhower, Assistant Chief of Staff, Operations Division (OPD), directed the commanding generals of the AAF and Eastern Defense Command (EDC) to do everything to improve antisubmarine operations by the First Air Force and the EDC to cooperate in solving problems with maintenance, supply, communications, the development of antisubmarine weapons, tactics, and techniques and that all B-18s would have radar installed. General Arnold requested that I Bomber Command needed reorganization to fulfill the unique requirements of antisubmarine and Allied air operations. It would be the Army's responsibility to operate in support of, or instead of, naval forces, to protect shipping.

General George C. Marshall supported the establishment of an antisubmarine command, and that of a centralized command was essential to the overall efficiency of antisubmarine operations:

General George C. Marshall, Army Chief, in 1946. He became a proponent of an Army Air Force Antisubmarine Command. (United States Army Center of Military History)

> The effective employment of air forces against submarines demands rapid communication, mobility, and freedom of restrictions inherent in command systems based upon areas of

responsibility… The Command will be charged with submarine destruction as its primary mission. Communications and base facilities will be provided to permit the direct transmission of necessary information and to ensure essential mobility.[5]

Again, the Army supported naval forces and did not address the unity of command or jurisdiction of antisubmarine operations. It only recognized that the AFF would engage in the mission and not just for emergencies. He held that although the unity of command is vested in the Navy, the Army must prepare to submit recommendations and take every action to make antisubmarine warfare fully effective. He recognized that the Navy held overall command, and the Army was subordinate to that service. Still, the Army would develop strategies and tactics to engage U-boats. However, in all intent and purpose, the AAF embarked upon establishing a separate organization from the Navy. US Army generals Omar Bradley and Westside T. Larson drew up plans clarifying the Army's antisubmarine command presented in a conference with General Eisenhower. Two of four principles consisted of the following:

- The unity of command is the fundamental principle upon which successful antisubmarine warfare must rest. The submarine possesses great mobility; successful action against it necessitates the elimination of overlapping jurisdiction so that prompt action may be facilitated. Command channels must be direct, and the "maddening and intolerable" system of verbal orders from one office and written orders from another be eliminated… A successful antisubmarine force must be able to move units from point to point to meet the requirements of a shifting situation.
- A "Coastal Air Force" should be organized with the I Bomber Command as its nucleus. The chain of command then would be from the Commanding General, AAF, to the Commanding General, Coastal Air Force Controller, to the Squadron Commander. An operations control room would be set up at each base, and steps would be taken to establish adequate intelligence coordination with the Navy. The Navy would, however, no longer exercise direct operational control over Army planes because all orders would pass through Headquarters Coastal Air Force.[6]

General Bradley prepared an additional plan for the conference that all but eliminated the Navy's overall control of the antisubmarine mission in which he called for I Bomber Command or a Coastal Air Force to protect coastal shipping under the direct control of a commanding general of the First Air Force. Furthermore, all Army and Navy aircraft would fall under the direct command of an Army officer. He added that all other cooperation between the Army and Navy would be by coordination rather than by unity of command, which was the case between the Eastern Defense Command and Eastern Sea Frontier. In so much, the Navy would only play a supporting role while the Army would take the leading role in ASW.

The Army additionally called for a strategic doctrine to combat the U-boat menace. In contrast, the Navy took on a defensive role, one in which protection of convoys was crucial. The Army argued that a well-coordinated offensive by aircraft and surface vessels could drive enemy submarines hundreds of miles from the coast, thus restricting their operations against shipping.

To further develop the Army's antisubmarine doctrine, British Coastal Command personnel were detailed to aid the Americans. Air Marshall Philip Joubert de la Ferté of Coastal Command, RAF, voiced his opinion on an offensive plan to combat U-boats: "The primary method of defeating the U-boat is to seek and strike. The greater portion of the air available should always be engaged in the direct attack of U-boats and the smallest possible number in immediate protection of shipping. Our experience is that a purely defensive policy only leads to heavy loss in merchant shipping."[7]

Once again, in 1942, the Navy possessed no long-range bombers and could not engage in an offensive U-boat campaign. Such a plan would contradict its doctrine of a defensive antisubmarine capacity in protecting coastal shipping. The Navy feared losing its role in ASW, if the Army undertook responsibility for the antisubmarine campaign if left unchecked. Admiral King believed that Army and Navy aircraft would remain under the control of respective sea frontiers. He, therefore, reinforced that all air units engaged in antisubmarine operations would fall under naval command and engage in defensive operations to protect coastal shipping. Accordingly, the Navy would continue to employ all available forces in the antisubmarine war. Thus the Navy and all other agencies concerned must continue intensifying the antisubmarine effort.

By the middle of March 1942, the situation remained severe when U-boats sank 85 ships, totaling more than 452,000 gross tons, primarily off the Eastern Seaboard, Newfoundland, Greenland, and Iceland, including 22 British tankers. Only a handful of medium-range planes based in Greenland and Iceland were available between January and March 1942. While the Army and Navy argued over jurisdiction and unity of command, shipping losses continued to climb at such an alarming rate that General Marshall expressed to Admiral King in June that "another month or two" of similar losses would "cripple our means of transport that we will be unable to bring sufficient men and planes against the enemy in critical theaters to exercise a determining influence on the war."[8]

Air Marshall Philip Joubert de la Ferté (left) of the English Coastal Command sought the American Air Force to begin offensive operations against German submarines. (Author's collection)

The United States military, at the time, was engaged in a defensive war with the Japanese, with the loss of Guam, Wake Island, and the Philippines. Consequently, there were limited resources to fight a two-ocean war at the time, and Admiral King understood that. The Army meanwhile saw the U-boat as a greater menace as the economic lifeline between the United States, the UK, and Russia was in peril of being cut. However, the Navy's Chief of Naval Operations observed that the United States could not devote all resources to fighting submarines while deferring the rest of the war to the future when it would be easier to undertake such a mission.

Problems remained, including the need for better-trained personnel and suitable aircraft fitted with radar for antisubmarine patrolling. The Army Air Force continued to deal with the Navy's defensive coastal doctrine and had no defined legal authority as Bomber Command performed such operations in supporting naval forces. Theoretically, the command could withdraw from the mission and return to its regular commitment of bombardment. Moreover, a unified Army/Navy command system had yet to be established.

Moreover, actual communication between the Eastern Sea Frontier and the Army Air Force proved troublesome. It was only possible by telephone or walking from one operation's room to another. An unknown individual described it as a waste of time and a source of irritation to personnel working in such a high pressure workplace. The British Coastal Command had a bitter experience with such operational procedure during the first two years of the war: Complete and unrestricted interchange of information or intelligence under the present poor physical set-up must again depend upon a telephone call, a messenger, or a visit from one operation room to another. The time and effort this involves can lead only to the eventual incomplete distribution of information.[9]

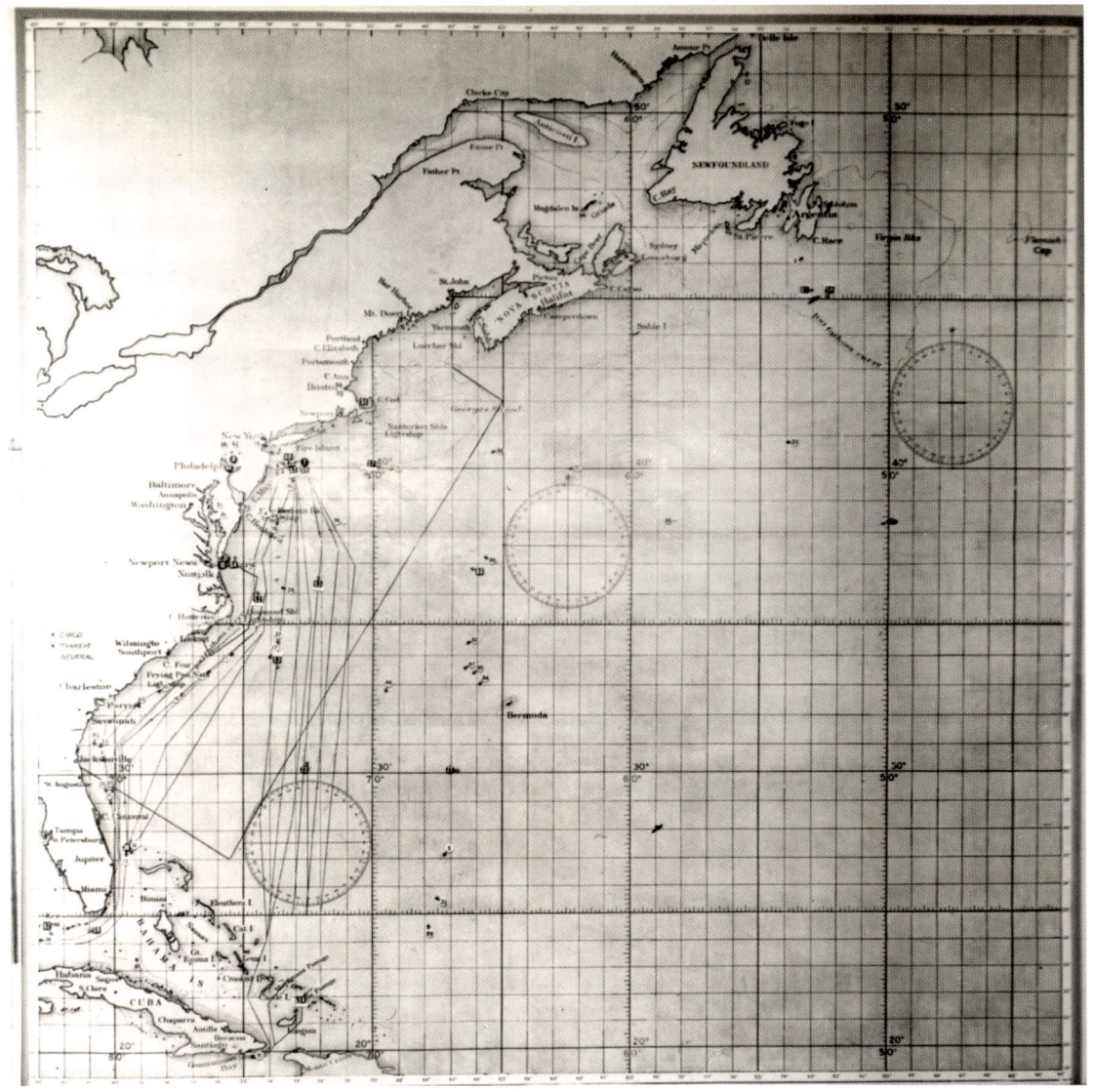

This wall chart in the naval control room measuring 18 x 17ft (5.48 by 5.18m) and shows the coastal shipping lanes of the Eastern Sea Frontier. (AFHRA Reel A4067, 2300)

By May 1942, six months of experience in U-boat hunting began to pay dividends as the number of attacks by Army and Navy units began increasing. Army aircraft flew 59,248 hours between January and October 1942, with 200 U-boat sightings and 81 attacks destroying four U-boats and severely damaging six. Yet the first American ship to sink a U-boat was by a US naval aircrew when it encountered and sank U-*656* under the command of 37-year-old Korvettenkapitän Ernst Kröning off Newfoundland on 1 March 1942. Naval aircraft would sink two more German submarines between February and June 1942, U-*503* and U-*158*, the last just a month before the AAF embarked on a successful antisubmarine crusade in the Caribbean between July 1942 and August 1943.

The communications office staffed by US naval personnel plotted coastal shipping lanes and perceived information on the location of U-boats. This office collaborated with Army and Navy assets to locate and attack German submarines. However, this collaboration caused delays and confusion in communications from this office to individual Army squadrons. This wall plot shows the last known positions of German submarines. (AFHRA Reel A4067, 225)

Dr Edward L. Bowles, technical advisor to the Assistant Secretary of War, urged the establishment of an Air Antisubmarine Force with the Navy's overall command. Still, the force would act as an independent agency with a general officer commanding the entire land-based component, including the Navy's; local command of such forces would cease to exist. General Marshall took the first step in forming such a command in a letter dated September 14, 1942, to Admiral King. "Experience with the First Bomber Command in antisubmarine operations since March indicates that the effective employment of air forces against the submarine demands rapid communications, mobility, and freedom from restrictions inherent in command systems based upon the area of responsibility."[10]

King saw Bowles' letter as a concerted effort for the Army to take complete control of antisubmarine operations and to expand it as an offensive tool. At the same time, the Chief of Naval Operations continued to push for antisubmarine activities to follow a defensive doctrine. In a letter to Lord Halifax in August 1942, he added that protecting convoys was essential to air operations. Yet, he saw an offensive strategy as the key to destroying the U-boat menace, something the US Navy was against. He said: "…

The Air Controller's duty for the AAF and the Navy was prompt and vigorous action upon all enemy contact reports. However, the Air Controllers were extremely slow in sending reports to individual Army antisubmarine units. (AFHRA Reel A4067, 220)

the primary method of defeating the U-boat is to seek and strike. The more significant portion of the air available should always be engaged in the direct attack of U-boats and the smallest possible number in the direct protection of shipping. Our [the British] experience is that a purely defensive policy only leads to heavy loss in merchant shipping."[11]

U-boat sightings increased as aircraft and crews became available, allowing for increased convoy coverage. The number of U-boat sightings and the number of shipping losses in the areas covered by I Bomber Command started to fall in July 1942 as more surface and air assets became available, as shown in the following table:

USAAF Antisubmarine Effort

I Bomber Command Area of Responsibility (Jan-Oct 1942)

Month	Aircraft Patrols	Ships Sunk	Submarines Sighted	Submarine Attacks
January	300	10	10	7
February	600	12	12	12
March	1250	32	27	26
April	1930	25	30	26
May	2100	51	23	12
June	1650	33	41	29
July	1950	20	23	16
August	1850	20	14	8
September	1800	1	14	2
October	1750	0	2	1

Source: *US Army*, Monthly Report, October 1942 (Army Air Forces Antisubmarine Command, 1943, 6–8).

Creation of I Bomber Command

Above left: The SS *Robert C. Tuttle* afire off Cape Henry, Virginia, on June 22, 1942. The *Tuttle* entered into a minefield laid by U-*701* off Virginia Beach. (NARA 80-G-14047)

Above right: SS *Santore* capsized and sank off the Chesapeake Capes, Virginia, after striking a German mine on June 17, 1942. The mine was laid on June 12 by submarine U-*701*. (NARA 80-G-63470)

First Kill

While the Army and Navy argued about the question of command and control, the first successful attack by an AAF plane against a German submarine occurred on July 7, 1942, when U-*701*, a type VIIC U-boat, commanded by Kapitänleutnant Horst Degan was found in the North Atlantic off Cape Hatteras, North Carolina, and sunk by an A-29 Hudson of the 396th Bombardment Squadron, 41st Bomb Group. Lieutenant Arthur H. Tuttle, piloting a B-17E, first sighted U-*701*, surfaced and laid six 325lb depth bombs across the submarine's bow. The depth bombs detonated and an estimated 150ft (45.7m) diameter oil slick was observed, which must have damaged the vessel. Tuttle stayed in the area until he was relieved by Lieutenant Harry J. Kane of the same bomb group, operating a Lockheed A-29 Hudson.

The Lockheed A-29 Hudson produced approximately 15 aircraft variants beginning in December 1938. The light bomber and reconnaissance model had a crew of five with a maximum speed of 246mph (396km/h), a surface ceiling of 25,000ft (7,600m), a range of 1,960 miles (3,150km), a maximum bomb load of 1,400lb (640kg), and was armed with two .303 machine guns in the dorsal turret and two .303 guns in the nose. Its overall length was 44ft (13.41m) with a wingspan of 65ft. (National Museum of the Air Force, 051122-F-1234P-015)

Lieutenant Kane spotted the boat and attacked using tactics the AFF and the British Coastal Command had taught him. He was flying a routine patrol from Chery Point, N.C. when he sighted a submarine seven miles away upon relieving Tuttle. Heavy cloud cover obscured his plane as Kane attacked from 50 feet, releasing three Mk XVII depth charges in a train for approximately 20 seconds after the submarine submerged. The submarine was still visible underwater as the bombs fell. The plane made two direct hits, the pressure hull was torn open, and water poured in. Bubbles appeared on the surface as one of U-*701*'s men appeared, followed by 15 more; seven of its 46-man crew survived, including Degan. In his interrogation, Degan stated that only one aircraft attacked; whether he was mistaken is open to interpretation. Lt. Kane's success resulted from accumulated experience, coaching from the British, improved depth bombs, installing radar such as the SCR-517, and using D/F gear, resulting in higher success levels. In the previous quarter, only seven of 54 attacks resulted in damage to submarines, but in the third quarter, eight of 24 attacks reportedly damaged submarines, not counting the one sunk on July 7.

A few months later, Arnold argued before the Joint Chief of Staff on October 19, 1942, that a new antisubmarine unit should be free to move as a killer-hunt group to operate in conjunction with, but not under the command of, the local Navy sector commander. By October 1942, the AAF began to move rapidly to establish offensive ASW operations by deploying two B-24 squadrons to work with British Coastal Command. On 3 November, the First Antisubmarine Squadron left Langley Field for duty in England to conduct offensive operations with British Coastal Command. The plan approved by the Joint Chiefs of Staff called for a sizeable force consisting of 288 heavy and 123 medium bombers, with this significant bomber force primarily consisting of B-24s. General Westside T. Larson recommended a force comprised of 42 squadrons with a total of 544 B-24 bombers operating from bases in the North Atlantic, the United Kingdom, Africa, South America, the Antilles, the Pacific Coast, India, Asia, Hawaii, and Russia. The AAF scaled down his request only to include the United Kingdom, the Eastern United States, the Caribbean, and the Mediterranean for the purpose of creating a highly mobile striking force with 19 squadrons equipped primarily with B-24s and B-25s. The actual number of squadrons formed for antisubmarine duty would eventually reach 25.

Possibly U-*701* at Kiel, Germany, circa 1941. The submarine became the first U-boat sunk by a USAAF during World War Two in the Atlantic Theater. (Author's collection).

Above left: The US Coast Guard rescues U-701 survivors after the U-boat sank off Cape Hatteras, North Carolina. (Naval History and Heritage Command NH96587)

Above right: There were seven survivors from U-701, including the Captain, Horst Degen. German sailor Mechanikersegefreiter Bruno Faust is lifted aboard a Coast Guard vessel. (Official US Coast Guard photograph, now in the collections of the National Archives 26-G-102143-5)

Below: Rescue of survivors from U-701 after being picked up by a US Coast Guard plane on July 7, 1942. (Courtesy of Jerry Mason, U-boat Archives)

Chapter 3
Formation of First Antisubmarine Command

Dr Phillip M. Morse of the Antisubmarine Operations Research Group (ASWORG) strongly suggested that a significant change in the antisubmarine battles required passing from the defensive to the offensive. He said:

The plane is primarily an offensive weapon against U-boats, being premiant by its speed and ability to seek out the enemy. The surface vessel is, at present, less than one percent as efficient at finding submarines as the plane and is no more efficient at killing the sub once found. Its primary advantage over the aircraft is its staying power, essentially a defensive property: the surface vessel will always be the backbone of the convoy escort. The plane is also helpful as an escort. Still, it is a most inefficient use of its offensive capabilities: to hold it down to protect convoys that are not explicitly threatened.[1]

On September 8, 1942, General George C. Marshal of the Army sent a detailed letter to Admiral King with his views on establishing the formation of the First Antisubmarine Command. Experience with I Bomber Command since March 1942 indicated that the effective employment of the air forces, both Army and Navy, against submarines demanded rapid communication, mobility, and freedom from the restricting environment in a command system based upon areas of responsibility. He became convinced and directed that establishing the command would create a well-organized system using I Bomber Command assets, under Army Command, with centralized control while maintaining the Navy's ability to track enemy submarine movement and activities. Therefore, operational control would remain with the Navy when submarine activities remained along sea frontiers. General Marshall looked upon prompt action of all antisubmarine air forces to critical areas as essential to defeating U-boats. The proposal was to centralize control of the new command to increase mobility and destroy submarines in any area requiring rapid deployment. The proposal was for offensive antisubmarine warfare.

Admiral King replied to General Marshall's letter three days later, concurring with the plan for a new command and that sea frontier commanders would have operational control of all air units engaged

From left to right are Lord Halifax, General Marshall, and Admiral King, with Mr. Bernard M. Baruch, an advisor to President Roosevelt. (National Archives and Records Administration, 80-G-286654)

in the antisubmarine mission within their jurisdictions. The USAAF's next step toward establishing the antisubmarine command occurred on September 20 when Lt. General McNarney, now Deputy Chief of Staff, wrote to General Arnold establishing the Army's Antisubmarine Command. General McNarney's directive to Arnold outlined the command's creation in six bullet points for establishing an Antisubmarine Command.

- The first called for Arnold to take steps to organize using personnel and equipment from the I Bomber Command. The bomber command would be inactivated to do so.
- The newly established force would be called the First Antisubmarine Army Air Command.
- USAAF command would assist the Navy in protecting friendly shipping.
- General Arnold would provide the necessary facilities for rapid movement and employment of antisubmarine aircraft and develop training and means of accomplishing the mission.
- The First Antisubmarine Army Air Command would serve directly under Arnold's headquarters while antisubmarine operations fell under the operational control of the Navy. Here again, power fell to the Navy and not the Army.
- The Navy's Operations Division would be advised of the readjustment of existing priorities for the allocation of planes and, out the AAF in that determination.[2]

The plan of operations outlined above called for the Navy's operational control of all antisubmarine operations in the Eastern and Gulf of Mexico Frontiers. It called for the command to base air units permanently along those areas. It also became essential that available squadrons would be on detached service from the command headquarters in one or more theaters. This primary directive also stated that the command would provide operating rights at the bases required to accomplish its mission. It would prepare and submit to Army Air Force Headquarters for the adequate performance of the mission.

The Army's adamant desire to take the offensive against U-boats continued to create a schism between it and the Navy as that service continued to invest in defensive coverage of coastal shipping while stressing the need for B-24s based in Newfoundland to cover the most dangerous part of the journey by ships from US ports to Europe. By late 1942, shipping losses began declining, and the defense phase of antisubmarine warfare had passed as German submarines left the Eastern Sea Frontier. With the steady increase in the production of escort ships, aircraft began to pay dividends in supplying adequate convoy protection. According to the AAF, it was time to take the offensive.

The Air Force activated the Army Air Force Antisubmarine Command (AAFASC) on 15 October 1942, followed by the deactivation of I Bomber Command. Upon activation of the Antisubmarine Command, it reported 209 operational aircraft at its disposal, and only 20 were B-24s. The AAFASC reported the availability of 125 B-17Es, B-18s, B-25s, B-34s, A-29s, and observation aircraft. Squadrons of the 25th and 26th Antisubmarine Command began operations to protect the Eastern Seaboard of the United States, the Gulf of Mexico, and the Caribbean against U-boat attacks. The Antisubmarine command established 25 antisubmarine squadrons under the 25th and 26th Air Wings from existing bombardment squadrons. Those consisting of the following: 25th Air Wing squadrons consisting of: 1st, 2nd, 3rd, 4th, 5th, 6th, 11th, 12th, 13th, 14th, 16th, 18th, 19th, 20th, 22nd, and 24th. The 26th Air Wing squadrons consisted of: 7th, 8th, 9th, 10th, 15th, 17th, 21st, 23rd, and 25th.

25th Antisubmarine Wing Commanders
Col. Harry A. Halverson (November 20, 1942)
Col. Howard Moore (November 20, 1942)
Col. Harry A. Halverson (November 20, 1942)
Col. Wallace E. Whitson (December 22, 1942)

Col. Chester A. Charles (June 8, 1943)
Col. Ephraim M. Hampton (August 20, 1943)

26 Antisubmarine Groups Commanding Officers
479th   Lt. Col. Howard Moore
480th   Lt. Col. Jack Roberts
26th Wing   Col. Harry A. Halverson (date unknown)

Location of Antisubmarine Command airfields along the Eastern Seaboard circa 1942–43. Air Force Historical Research Agency (AFHRA) at Maxwell AFB. (AFHRA Reel A4070, 350)

A month later, in November 1942, the 1st and 2nd Antisubmarine Squadrons, equipped with B-24Ds, were ordered to England from Langley Field, Virginia. Six of the 25 squadrons established would serve in England or Morrocco. At the same time, similarly equipped units would operate along the East Coast, the Gulf of Mexico, the Caribbean, and Newfoundland. B-24s of the 1st and 2nd Antisubmarine Squadron planes were equipped primarily with the SCR-517C radar for locating surfaced German submarines. They were initially dispatched to the United Kingdom to train in Coastal Command ASW methods; however, the British urgently needed VLR aircraft. Therefore, the AAF decided to use the American squadrons to operate with Coastal Command, especially in the Bay of Biscay area.

The establishment of the AAFASC coincided with the change in German tactics from the Western to the North Atlantic and approaches to North Africa in preparation for an Allied offensive in Northern Africa. Hereto, the question remained on what branch had jurisdiction over VLR aircraft. Ultimately, it legitimized the Army's antisubmarine command but did nothing to solve the defensive versus offensive fence both services were sitting on.

Above left: A flight of B-17s based out of Mitchell Field. The plane closest has the ASW paint scheme, while the rear plane displays the olive drab scheme with s/n 19065. Note the aerial display on the aircraft's top rear and one protruding from the nose. (HFHRA Real A4088, 881) (AFHRA Reel A4088, 88)

Above right: A B-17, serial number (s/n) 12473, of the 3rd Antisubmarine Squadron, based at Mitchell Field, displays the radar dome and sports an antisubmarine warfare (ASW) paint scheme. Note the radar pod. (AFHRA Reel A4088, 888)

Below: B-24D, s/n 241047, of the 10th Antisubmarine Squadron based in Galveston, Texas. (AFHRA Reel A4088, 853)

A pair of B-24D Liberators belonging to an unknown antisubmarine squadron, possibly at Mitchell Field, Virginia. Note the plane on the left's rear turret area. (AFHRA Reel A4088, 860)

An unusual B-24D, s/n 241107, from an unknown USAAF ASW squadron with squadron letter G, possibly based at Mitchell Field, New York. (AFHRA Reel A4088, 870)

B-25 Mitchells of the 3rd Antisubmarine Squadron with the "Bat Out of Hell" squadron emblem. The squadron was activated at Langley Field, Virginia, and based at Fort Dix, New Jersey, in April 1943. The squadron was initially formed as the 39th Bombardment Squadron (Medium) on November 20, 1940, and became the 3rd Antisubmarine Squadron in November 1942. The squadron became the 819th Bombardment Squadron (Heavy) in September 1943. (Air Force Historical Research Agency, Heraldry Program)

Above left: The "Bat Out of Hell" emblem of the 3rd Antisubmarine Squadron. In June 1943, the 3rd Squadron began operations out of Orlando Army Air Field, Florida. (Air Force Historical Research Agency, Heraldry Program)

Above right: A closer view of the 5th Squadron emblem shows a clenched fist holding a four-prong lightning bolt on a white disc encircled in blue. (AAF)

Below: A B-25 of the 5th Antisubmarine Squadron performed ASW duty along the Eastern Coast. The squadron was activated in November 1942 and was based at Westover Field, Massachusetts. In September 1943, it became the 829th Bombardment Squadron. (AFHRA Reel 4088, 889)

B-25, s/n 112820, of the 5th Antisubmarine Squadron, with the squadron emblem under the co-pilot's station and the name *SEMINOLE* painted under the side of the plexiglass nose. (AFHRA Reel A4088, 874)

Above left: A B-24D Liberator, s/n 241231, of the 13th Antisubmarine Squadron based at Grenier Field, New Hampshire, sporting the squadron emblem below the cockpit. The squadron was first organized as the 518th Bombardment Squadron, later the 863rd Bombardment Squadron, and was renamed the 13th Antisubmarine Squadron in November 1942. (AFHRA Reel A4088, 871)

Above right: A closer view of the aircraft in the previous image shows the cat emblem below the pilot's station.

Left: The emblem of the 13th Antisubmarine Squadron/863rd Bombardment. It's a light blue disc with dark blue water within black and orange keylines. It incorporates a winged black cat with a yellow face, red tongue, white paws, and an elongated tail, riding an aerial torpedo of orange with a shark's face, all emitting speed lines of white. A white cloud tops the emblem. The AAF approved it on May 13, 1943. (Air Force Historical Research Agency, Heraldry Program)

A B-25 Mitchell of the 16th Antisubmarine Squadron, s/n 30143, based in Charlestown, South Carolina. Its predecessor was the 820th Bombardment Squadron, which was redesignated as the 16th Antisubmarine Squadron in November 1942. In September 1943, the squadron was inactivated and became the 820th Bombardment Squadron that same month. (AFHRA Reel A4088, 851)

Above left: A closeup of the 16th Antisubmarine Squadron emblem on the Mitchell. The emblem was that of Alley Oop, a newspaper cartoon figure popular at the time. He is grasping a red stone club with a green handle in his right hand and hurling an aerial bomb in his left hand. (AFHRA Reel A4088, 851)

Above right: The official emblem for the 18th Antisubmarine, which later became the 4th Search Operational Training Squadron for the 1st Antisubmarine Command. It is characterized as having waves with a black periscope pierced by a silver sword with a red hilt. (Air Force Historical Research Agency, Heraldry Program)

Unresolved Questions

With the creation of I Bomber Command and afterward, the AAFASC attempted to function as a legitimate antisubmarine force that could take on U-boats offensively. At the same time, the Navy continued to argue for a defensive war to protect coastal shipping convoys. In so much, the services argued over conflicting strategies and the multiple commands. Albert V. Alexander, First Lord of the Admiralty, stated, "I would emphasize that aircraft, specially adapted and with crews specially trained for work over the sea, are an essential component of the forces required under modern conditions of the exercise of sea power." Again, as did the AAF, he and others wanted to conduct offensive antisubmarine warfare. Still, Admiral King's position did not waver as the Atlantic Convoy Conference between March 1 and 12, 1943, in Washington, DC, hoped to resolve the question. Representatives of the Navy, the AAF, the War Shipping Administration, the Royal Air Force, the Royal Navy, and the Royal Canadian Navy attended. Here, Admiral King spoke defensively and voiced his concerns regarding expanding antisubmarine operations as an offensive tool, explaining that the Army was ignoring the overall plans; the situation in the Pacific probably preoccupied King's mind and that additional aircraft would be required in that theater due to the potentialities of the Japanese undertaking submarine warfare on par with the Germans, thus threatening shipping on the West Coast and threatening the Panama Canal. He added that limited antisubmarine resources would provide a defensive means to maintain the flow of shipping that is essential to the general aims of the war. Except for American naval officers in attendance, he had no supporters regarding his defensive doctrine. In the meeting, the British and Canadian counterparts emphasized the need for an offensive campaign against enemy submarines. Admiral Sir Percy Noble, British Royal Navy, said that the U-boat menace is:

> Becoming more and more an air problem every day. We haven't had enough aircraft during the last two years. We are just reaching a point where we can see ahead of us the chance of getting enough, and I am sure this conference will come to some agreements and decisions as to how to best use those aircraft when we get them and when they get to their proper operational theaters.[3]

Although overall shipping losses for July through October 1942 were significant, with 426 vessels sunk or damaged in all areas, the Western Atlantic saw a continued decrease as the German submarine command shifted U-boats to other areas where they continued to wreak havoc. However, there would not be an overall downturn in shipping losses until mid-1943—resulting from the increased availability of surface and air units with trained personnel. By early 1943, Admiral King held on to the defensive positions and expressed, "Let us say, by way of emphasis, that the remainder of 1943, at least, must concern itself primarily with the escort of convoys." Admiral Noble, head of the British Admiralty Delegation in Washington, followed Admiral King to remind him that shipping was the most critical factor in the successful prosecution of the whole war. Too much shipping is in danger of being destroyed. King added, "At this moment, the situation is causing anxiety, and the submarine menace is becoming more and more of an air problem every day. They have not had enough aircraft during the last two years."[4]

Admiral King did not oppose using aircraft for antisubmarine operations; he opposed extending their use for offensive purposes because of limited resources. Moreover, he wasn't opposed to creating killer groups when the Army and Navy had the necessary means to do so to protect shipping along the coastal waters. He added, "I see no profit in searching the ocean or even any but a limited area, such as a focal area…antisubmarine warfare must concern itself primarily with the escort of convoys." Once again, the AAF and Navy had competing strategies for the best antisubmarine warfare method. If anything, the conference solidified opposing strategies and ASW's command, making it complicated to embark upon a concrete, unified command structure. The meeting did little to attempt to standardize communications, intelligence dissemination, training, and tactical doctrine.[5]

Sir Percy Noble (center) and staff in December 1941. He was the commanding officer of the western approaches to the Atlantic Ocean. (Author's collection, unknown origin)

It did underscore the importance of aviation in antisubmarine warfare. Still, Admiral King and AAF staff were at an impasse regarding creating an organization that would meet their demands. According to AFF members, however, it seems that Navy members "interposed strenuous objections" to any plans that amounted to a change in their existing organization or policies. The Army, entrenched in its position, continued to seek an independent force for offensive operations by utilizing a fast, mobile striking force deployed to areas with a high concentration of U-boats. King offered his advice to protect shipping by conducting defensive warfare with limited resources. He added:

> I have heard something about "killer groups," which may be of great use when we can get enough means, provided they are used directly in connection with the convoy routes, for that is where "bait" is. I see no profit in searching the ocean, or even any but a limited area, such as focal areas–all else puts to shame the proverbial search for a needle in a haystack...antisubmarine warfare for the remainder of 1943, at least, must concern itself primarily with the escort of convoys.[6]

The question regarding control of antisubmarine operations began to turn in the Army Air Force's favor during the Allied Conference in January 1943 at Casablanca, French Morocco, when Great Britain and the United States agreed to deploy B-24 aircraft to patrol the mid-Atlantic gap. The British immediately began operating B-24s from bases in Ireland and Iceland to cover the eastern part of the gap. Still, the US Navy did not dispatch any aircraft to protect the western stretches of the mid-Atlantic. During February 1943, 22 ships totaling almost 200,000 tons were lost, mainly in the western gap. The following month, the Allies lost 38 ships of 750,000 tons and an escort in four convoys crossing the Atlantic.

Rear Admiral Francis S. Low, United States Navy (USN), served as Assistant Chief of Staff for antisubmarine warfare. (Naval History and Heritage Command 80-G-302311)

On March 18, a B-24 detachment of the 25th Antisubmarine Wing established a headquarters at St. John's, Newfoundland. After negotiations involving the Army, Navy, British, and Canadian representatives, the 25th Antisubmarine Wing established headquarters in Gander, Newfoundland, under the command of Colonel Howard Moore. The 19th Antisubmarine Squadron, equipped with B-17s and B-24s, arrived in March, followed by the 6th Antisubmarine Squadron a few weeks later.

Unity of command continued through the first half of 1943. A report (OPS 56/3, dated March 1, 1943) recommended the antisubmarine effort headed by one naval commander who would concentrate exclusively on the antisubmarine effort in areas the operation clearly defined for the two services. The Army voiced descent as the report said nothing about offensive antisubmarine operations. To solidify the Navy's position, on May 20, 1943, Admiral King established the Tenth U.S. Fleet with a centralized antisubmarine command; commanded by Admiral King himself with Rear Admiral Francis S. Low, the latter as chief-of-staff. The mission consisted of coordinating and directing naval forces in the Battle of the Atlantic by the destruction of enemy submarines; the protecting Allied shipping in the Eastern, Gulf, and Caribbean Sea Frontiers, the exercise of convoy shipping as the United States' responsibility and the correlation between United States antisubmarine training and material development training.

The Army and Navy reached a final decision at a conference held on June 10, 1943, by General Arnold, General McNarney, and Rear Admiral John S. McCain. In brief, the AAF would no longer participate in antisubmarine operations, thus freeing up Army aircraft and personnel for strategic bombing based on some of the following criteria:

- The Navy is requested to submit a schedule on which the Army can turn over its planes to the Navy and draw up the need for replacement planes.
- The Air Force agreed to turn over antisubmarine operations to the Navy with the provision that the Navy would not participate in strategic bombing. The Army would withdraw Army Air Forces from antisubmarine duty when the Navy prepared to undertake such responsibilities.
- The Navy's Sixth Air Wing will contain no striking forces but would be restricted to airplanes capable of undertaking such offshore striking forces to defend the western hemisphere for active operations in other theaters and will be assigned an Army responsibility.
- Long-range patrol planes assigned to Fleet Air Wings are for the primary purpose of conducting offshore patrol, relieving the Army for strategic striking forces from this duty.[7]

General Marshall sent Admiral King a letter agreeing it was time for the Navy to undertake ASW operations. On June 28, Marshall sent a letter to Admiral King supporting Arnold, McNarney, and McCain's proposal. It would take several months before the Navy could field ASW squadrons, with some AAF units taking until November 1943 before being relieved. Before then, the AAF conducted ASW operations, with limited success, between July 1942 and August 1943, with the first occurring on July 6, 1942, in the Caribbean.

Chapter 4
Caribbean Operations (1942–43)

Before Pearl Harbor, the United States held a small number of Navy PBY Catalinas and AAF planes in the Caribbean, with naval and army facilities located in Panama, Cuba, and Puerto Rico, with successful negotiations allowing the use of Britain's overseas territories of Antigua, Barbados, British Guyana, Jamaica, and Trinidad, while the Dutch allowed the use of its territories in the West Indies. The Caribbean Defense Command, established in early 1941, preceded the Caribbean Sea Frontier (CARIBSEAFRON) with the purpose of defending the Caribbean, Central America, Venezuela, Columbia, Ecuador, and French Guinea. On December 22, 1941, Major General Frank M. Andrews, Commanding General of the Caribbean Defense Command, issued Directive No. 1, creating an air task force of all bombardment aviation in Panama Sector, Caribbean Defense Command, including all Navy patrol bomber aviation assigned to the Caribbean Air Force. The mission was to establish aerial reconnaissance patrols of the Pacific and Atlantic sectors of the Panama Coastal Sector and to locate, trail, and attack enemy forces encountered in the region.

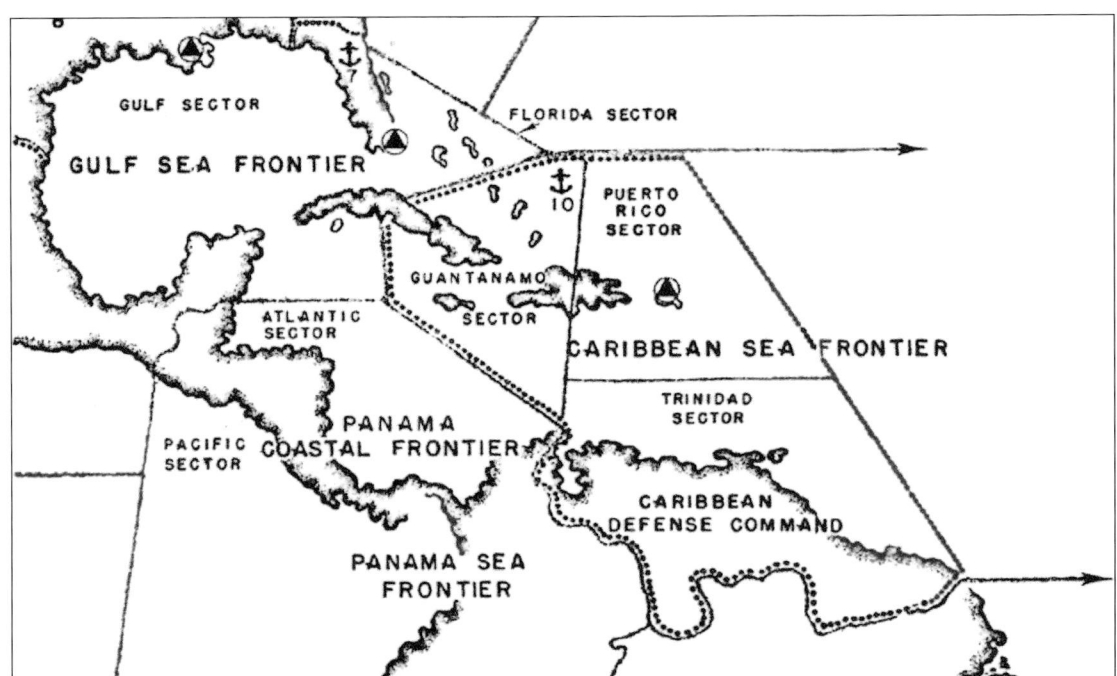

This is a map of the Caribbean Sea Frontier with subsections in 1942. In February 1942, U-boats began operations in the area. (AFHRA Reel A4070 349)

Above left: In November 1940, Lieutenant General Frank Andrews was assigned to command the Panama Canal Zone and extended to include command of Caribbean military forces circa August 1941. (USAF 1942190520-F-ZZ966-1522)

Above middle: Major General Davenport Johnson assumed the role of commanding general of the Caribbean Defense Force and 6th Air Force on August 9, 1941. (USAF 90212-F-ZZ966-1533)

Above right: Lieutenant General George H. Brett relieved General Davenport Johnson in November 1942. He remained the Caribbean Defense Force's and Panama's commanding officer through the war's end. (USAF 90212-F-ZZ966-1533)

U-boat Activity in the Caribbean

Admiral Dönitz began shifting some of his U-boat forces farther south to the Gulf of Mexico and the Caribbean beginning in February 1942. Shipping was plentiful, and sailed relatively safely in southern waters. Dönitz knew it and formed Operation *Neuland (New Ground),* with operations concentrating around Trinidad, owing to its proximity to Venezuela's oil fields, the bauxite mines in Dutch Guiana, and petroleum manufacturing facilities on the Dutch islands of Curacao and Aruba. Between February and July 1942, U-boats accounted for the loss of 114 merchantmen. *Operation Neuland* began when U-*156*, under the command of Kapitänleutnant Werner Hartenstein, arrived outside San Nicholas harbor of Aruba on the evening of February 15, 1942. The well-lit shoreline outlined several oil-laden tankers. Torpedoes slammed into the 4,300-ton British tanker *Pedernales,* followed moments later by the 2,400-ton tanker *Oranjestad*. Oil from the torn hauls poured out of the ship and quickly ignited, causing massive flames to spread across the water. The 6,400-ton American tanker *Arkansas* became the next victim of U-*156*'s torpedoes, with its cargo of crude oil adding to the inferno.[1]

In late February, Kapitänleutnant Asmus Nicolai Clausen's U-*129* arrived in the Caribbean. It sank seven merchantmen during two weeks beginning on 20 February. His first victim was the Norwegian freighter *Nordvangen*, followed by the Canadian freighter *George L. Torain* and the American *West Zeda* two days later. Clausen ended the month by sinking the Panamanian freighter *Bayou* on the 28th. Twenty-four ships, a majority of them tankers, totaling more than 118,000 tons, fell to U-boats during the first month of operations in the Caribbean. The arrival of enemy submarines increased the urgency as it became apparent by the end of February that a full assault by enemy submarines had materialized. During the first month of operations in February 1942, German submarines sank 24 vessels in the Caribbean Frontier with 240,000 gross tons. May and June saw the number of ships lost reach 124. During the height of the U-boat blitz in the Caribbean, Gulf of Mexico, and Panama sea frontiers in June 1942, 66 ships were lost, with a total tonnage of 314,000 tons.[2]

Caribbean Sea Frontier Merchant Shipping Losses in 1942

Month	Ships	Gross Tons
January	0	0
February	24	118,354
March	17	99,481
April	14	Not available
May	58	255,143
June	66	314,562
July	28	132,110
August	46	241,368
September	32	133,450
October	16	65,927
November	25	149,077
December	10	49,950
Total	336	1,559,422

Source: Stetson Conn, *Guarding the United States and its Outposts: The Caribbean in Wartime*, Ch. XVI (2000).

Above: Ships underway in the Caribbean Sea during World War Two. (Naval History and Heritage Command, UA 556.01 W.H. Saunders Collection)

Right: SS *Esso Bolivar* was damaged by shellfire from U-*126* in the Caribbean on March 8, 1942. (Naval History and Heritage Command NH 54112)

Army Air Force Countermeasures

By May 1942, U-boat activity in the Caribbean increased sharply from 14 ships lost in April to 58 in May and 66 in June. The Army Air Force attempted to convince the Navy to shift additional I Bomber Command aircraft to the Caribbean area. Still, the Navy rejected the proposal, fearing U-boats would return to the Eastern and Western Atlantic in numbers. Early on, the Army and Navy could not formulate an effective strategy for ASW by aircraft and personnel, and this was highlighted when the one AAF unit that did transfer to the Caribbean experienced constant frustration. Part of the 40th Bombardment Squadron (Medium) stationed at Mitchell Field, NY, was assigned temporary duty in Cuba for ten days but was transferred several more times to the Caribbean, for an overall total of 74 days, as ordered by naval command. Moreover, the naval commanders at Vernam Field, Jamacia, Edinburg Field, Trinidad, San Juan, Puerto Rico, Zanderig Field, Surinam, Dutch Guiana, and Guantanamo Bay, Cuba, did not understand AAF equipment, training, and mode of operations. Meanwhile, the Navy provided little intelligence information and kept its communications traffic away from the AAF.

The bombardment groups available between 1941 and 1942 consisted of the Sixth (Heavy), Nineth (Heavy), 25th (Medium), and 40th (Medium). The VI Air Force would expand throughout the Caribbean and Latin America, scattered throughout the Caribbean in Trinidad, Curacao, Aruba, St. Lucia, Surinam, British Guiana, Puerto Rico, St. Croix, and Antigua. Yet, the primary mission was to defend the Panama Canal from attacks by the Germans or the Japanese; thus, personnel had little experience conducting ASW.

A B-17 over Panama heading towards the Caribbean Sea for antisubmarine duty. This aircraft was scrapped between 1946 and 1947. (National Archives and Records Administration, 42-FH-3A00524-60563AC)

VI Air Force Lineage
Panama Canal Air Force (established October 1940)
Caribbean Air Force (established August 1941)
VI Air Force (established February 1942)

In mid-June 1942, at the height of the U-boat blitz in the Caribbean, ten Army bombers were shifted from the Atlantic sector to complement 24 Catalina PBYs of the Navy's Patrol Wing Three (FAW-3) with four squadrons of the 40th Bombardment Group (Medium), operating B-17s and B-26s, moving to Panama to protect the canal. Air coverage during the spring and summer was relatively insignificant, with 28 bombers (15 equipped with ASV radar,) 30 medium bombers, 16 light bombers, 34 Navy PBY patrol bombers, and fighter and observation planes stationed on the Atlantic side of the Panama Canal. The high point of 216 planes of all types occurred in July 1942 as the U-boat menace reached its height in the Caribbean. By that time, only 28 aircraft had ASV radar installed.

The 26th Antisubmarine Wing, based in Miami, undertook operations off Cuba with the 8th, 15th, 17th, and 23rd Antisubmarine Squadrons, which were undertaking operations to guard Florida and the Gulf of Mexico. In the Trinidad area, the 7th, 8th, 9th, and 10th Antisubmarine Squadrons, operating under the 45th Bombardment Group, equipped with B-17s and B-25s, arrived at Edinburgh Field, Trinidad, with a flight from the 417th Bombardment Squadron. The First AAF Antisubmarine Command sent the 7th Antisubmarine

Above: A Panama Sea Frontier B-24 Liberator coming in to land in Panama circa 1943-44. (NARA 342-FH-3A49304-K1923)

Right: Operational briefing by the commanding officer on July 25, 1942, regarding the location of a reported submarine somewhere in the Caribbean Sea. (NARA 342-FH-3A49362A-K2004)

Armorers loading 250lb depth charges into the bomb bay of a B-25 Mitchell in Panama. (NARA 342-FH-3A49313-K1950)

Squadron, a section of the 25th Bombardment Group equipped and with B-18s, replaced the 9th Antisubmarine Squadron; the latter having had radar-equipped aircraft, flew 12 missions daily, and conducted unsuccessful contacts with German submarines. By July 1942, there were enough aircraft to establish a convoy system. By the end of September, the VI air force consisted of 44 heavy bombers, 65 medium bombers, 22 light bombers, and 105 observation planes, in addition to Navy PBYs and 53 Squadron, RAF, equipped with the Lockheed Hudson. Still, the arrival of such a force failed to stem the flow of merchant shipping losses, with 29 vessels totaling 136,400 tons sunk in the Caribbean, 13 in the Atlantic sector of the Panama Canal, and another 16 in the Gulf Sea Frontier. Yet, other Army Air Force units in the Caribbean saw intensive action, sinking three U-boats between July and October 1942.

The AAF Strikes Back

The first U-boat lost to USAAF air power in the Caribbean occurred on July 6, 1942, when an A-20 Havoc of the 59th Bombardment Squadron piloted by Lieutenant M.E. Groover and flying out of Edinburgh Field, sank the Type IXC U-*153* on its first combat patrol. Leaving Kiel in May 1942 after training, it barely survived a month and a half. Under the command of 37-year-old Fregattenkapitän (Frigate Captain) Wilfried Reichmann, U-*153* sank three ships off Haiti and South America before its loss northwest of Aruba, with the loss of all 52 men aboard. It was the first AAF kill in the Caribbean. Still, the destruction of enemy submarines by Army planes was intermittent, with two additional U-boats sunk on 22 August and 2 October 1942.

The second sinking occurred on 22 August when U-*654*, commanded by Oberleutnant (First Lieutenant) 26-year-old Ludwig Forster, was caught on the surface north of Colon in the Gulf of Panama by B-18 Bolos

An A-20 Havoc similar to the one used by the 45th Bombardment Squadron that sunk U-654. (Author's collection)

Above left: Possibly U-654 at Brest, France, sometime in 1941. (Author's Collection/unknown origination)

Above right: Ludwig Forster (center) is the commanding officer of the ill-fated U-654. The submarine was lost with all hands. (Author's collection)

Right: A B-18 Bolo in Panama in June 1942. The B-18 saw extensive antisubmarine service in the Caribbean with antisubmarine and bombardment squadrons. (NARA, 342-FH-3A00424-21167AC)

B-18 Bolo bombers from the 99th Bombardment Group over Dutch Guyana on their way to intercept a reported enemy submarine. (NARA 342-FH-3A00426-21363AC)

from the 45th Bombardment Squadron, 40th Bombardment Group. A prowling B-18 piloted by 1st Lt. Penev A. Koenig spotted the U-boat and its 44-man crew. Four depth bombs straggled it, causing mortal damage to the vessel and leaving a large oil slick. Soon afterward, other B-18s arrived with one plane's depth bombs landing near or on *U-654*, sending up debris and oil. A large air bubble, some ten feet in diameter, appeared 15 minutes later. There were no survivors as the vessel sank beneath the waves.

On 2 October, the last U-boat lost to a US Army plane occurred off South America when a B-18A piloted by Captain Howard Burhanna of the 99th Bombardment Squadron, 9th Bombardment Group, flying out of Zandry Field, Dutch Guiana, spotted Kapitänleutnant Wolfgang Schultze's Type VIIC *U-512* on the surface north of Cayenne, French Guiana. According to Francis Machon, the lone survivor of 49 men aboard *U-512*, Schultze was thoroughly disliked and mistrusted by his crew. They considered him vain, temperamental, and professionally incompetent, and the crew frequently grumbled over his tactical shortcomings. Schulze additionally preferred to fight on the surface against air attack. Schultze was inclined to stay on the surface during simulated attacks, firing at planes until he would order a crash dive, leaving men topside to swim without warning until the U-boat resurfaced. Machon, during his interrogation, recounted *U-512*'s demise. On the deck, smoking a cigarette, he said, I heard a cry, "Airplane dead ahead!" from the watch. The boat's radar was either not being monitored or out of commission. Schultze ordered a crash dive immediately, and five men on the deck tumbled down the hatch.[3]

At that point, Burhanna's plane dropped a string of depth bombs from 50 feet; two were direct hits. Water immediately rushed into the boat, and it settled rapidly. Schultz ordered the tanks blown in an attempt to resurface, only to continue sinking by the bow. The U-boat continued sinking, and the bow hit the bottom, followed by the stern. The boat then came to rest almost level and with no list at 137ft (42m). Francis Machon worked his way to the bow torpedo room and slammed a fire extinguisher against the bulkhead. He was let in and found 15 men waiting inside. Chlorine gas began filling the battery compartment, and the men began to cough. The men found only four escape lungs, and only one worked. Men began collapsing and coughing; some were bleeding from the ears and mouth from chlorine and high air pressure. Machon and a boatswain mate attempted to open the torpedo-loading hatch to escape instead of dying from the gas. They managed to escape, but the boatswain drowned during the ascent. Machon found the surface and treaded water for more than an hour before a circling plane dropped a life raft–his home for the next ten days. On October 12, the destroyer USS *Ellis* rescued him.

Against the morning sun, a B-18 medium bomber takes off for an antisubmarine hunt from an unknown airbase in the Caribbean. (NARA 342-FH-3A00425-213)

Caribbean Operations (1942–43)

After the sinking of U-*512*, the AAF did not sink another enemy submarine for the remainder of operations in the Caribbean. However, enemy submarines continued operating in the region as nuisances, sinking or damaging 83 merchant ships with a tally of more than 400,000 tons for the remainder of 1942. In November 1942, Dönitz began shifting his assets away from the Caribbean and the North Atlantic to the Mediterranean to counter the Allied invasion of North Africa under Operation *Torch*. Meanwhile, shipping losses in the Caribbean fell from 25 ships lost in November to 10 in December 1942. Operation *Torch*, the increasing number of naval and AAF aircraft, a steady growth in Allied surface vessels, and the distance U-boats had to travel from their home ports in France, undoubtedly influenced the strategic withdrawal of most U-boats from the Caribbean. However, Dönitz kept a token U-boat presence in the Caribbean, with Bombardment Squadrons 5th, 80th, and 417th recording attacks during the last months of 1942, while the 8th and 9th Antisubmarine Squadrons recorded seven attacks during 1943, with two submarines recorded as slightly damaged.

Captain Howard Burhanna, Jr. (standing far right) and his crew operating a B-18A Bolo, which sank U-*512* north of Cayenne, French Guiana. (NARA 342-FH-3A00435-3A00435)

Douglas B-18B (SN 37-530, originally a B-18A) with the Magnetic Anomaly Device tail boom that could detect submerged submarines. (NARA 342-FH-3A00429-23193AC)

Chapter 5
The 480th Antisubmarine Group

The first air group sent to the European Theater as an offensive antisubmarine unit, and initially named the 1st Antisubmarine Group (Provisional), formed at Langley Field, Virginia, in October 1942, originally from personnel of the 2nd Bombardment Group, 304th Bombardment Squadron. It had engaged in antisubmarine patrol and convoy coverage along the eastern coast and Newfoundland. Aircrews of the group picked up B-24Ds from the production line in Fort Worth, Texas. Afterwards, they flew to Patterson Field in Dayton, Ohio, to install radar before heading to Langley Field for overseas deployment. The 1st Antisubmarine Group (Provisional) would be renamed the 2037th Antisubmarine Wing (Provisional) in January 1943 and the 480th Antisubmarine Group in June 1943.

Left: AAF officers are in front of a B-24D ready for delivery in San Diego or Fort Worth. Note the coloration. (Alan Griffith Collection)

Below: A line-up of B-24Ds, or the Navy's PBY4-1, white on the front and top of the wings and olive drab on the upper surfaces. (Alan Griffith Collection)

Operations From England

The first elements of the 1st Antisubmarine Squadron, a detachment of the 25th Antisubmarine Wing, began arriving at St. Eval, England, in November 1942, only to find that no one knew anything about the squadron's arrival. There, the wing commander and commander of the 1st Antisubmarine Squadron, 31-year-old Lt. Colonel Jack Roberts, was mystified about what control the unit would operate under. After several discussions, the squadrons fell under Eighth Bomber Command for supply and administrative control and operationally under 19 Group, RAF. With the first echelon in place, subsequent aircraft and crews in Newfoundland found it challenging to cross the Atlantic. Six from the 1st Squadron left on November 23, 1942, and ran into severe turbulence and icy conditions, and only two made it across the Atlantic; the weather conditions forced back three, and one disappeared. At St. Eval on November 16, nine days after arriving with the first element. Isacc J. Haviland flew the first mission for the 1st Antisubmarine Squadron, and on December 29, Captain D.C. Northrup conducted the first but unsuccessful attack against a U-boat.

The 2nd Antisubmarine Squadron, formed from the 523rd Bombardment Squadron, reached England on January 12, 1943. Its arrival created the First Antisubmarine Group (Provisional) on January 15 and the 2037th Antisubmarine Wing on March 1. This squadron flew its first mission in European waters on January 16, 1942, only four days after reaching the UK. However, constant fog and rainy weather hampered operations during January, resulting in the deaths of First Lt. George O. Broussard and his crew of the 2nd Squadron when their plane hit a cliff on 22 January 1943. Operational missions were usually 11 to 17 hours long, and such long missions searching vast areas became fatiguing. The group arrived during the worst months of the year in the UK, resulting in personnel contracting bronchial infections. The weather and crew sickness created a three-day gap between missions due to physical and mental stress and for the men's best interest.

Lt. Colonel Roberts summed up the life of belonging to an antisubmarine group stating that crews must be watchful throughout missions that could last up to 17 hours. It was a different kind of warfare

Above left: Lt. Colonel Jack Roberts was the commanding officer of the 480th Antisubmarine Group. (AFHRA Reel A4070, 709)

Above right: Major Alfred J. Hanlon Jr. was the commanding officer of the 1st Squadron, 480th Antisubmarine Group. (AFHRA Reel A0522, 548)

St. Eval Air Base, where the 480th Antisubmarine Group was stationed between November 1942 to March 1943. (Author's collection)

than strategic bombing with defined land targets. The antisubmarine crew usually flew alone, and no one knew their fate, if lost. Thus, he said, antisubmarine crews were not exposed to the immense psychological comfort of wing-tip to wing-tip fellowship that other types of aerial warfare provide. Singly, they flew patrols over the Bay of Biscay and, later, the Mediterranean.

Bay of Biscay Offensive

The first Bay of Biscay offensive in which the Antisubmarine Command's squadrons participated in large numbers was the "Gondola" campaign of February 6–15, 1943. The bay acted as a transit point for U-boats leaving the French ports of Brest, Lorient, St. Nazaire, and La Pallice. All U-boats entering or leaving those ports had to funnel through the bay patrolled by Coastal Command aircraft. The bay covers a large area from France's west coast and Spain's north coast. It extends to Ushant Island off the coast of Brittany, France, and south to Cape Finisterre at the north-west tip of Spain. The body of water is small for patrolling aircraft, 300 miles from north to south and 120 miles from east to west.

By February, British Coastal Command began conducting large-scale operations over the bay. The 1st Antisubmarine Group was essential as it supplied two additional squadrons for Coastal Command due to the higher concentration of U-boats attempting to leave bases in France for open water in the Atlantic and Mediterranean. The campaign was a high-density patrol of all approaches to the Bay of Biscay using long-range B-24s by Coastal Command and the 1st and 2nd Squadrons equipped with radar. British and American antisubmarine units exploited the weakness of submarines having to recharge batteries, ventilate the vessel, and permit crew members topside for fresh air. The fight or flight strategy of remaining surfaced during the day allowed aircraft radar operators to home in on surfaced U-boats.

Operation *Gondola* Actions by the 1st Antisubmarine Group

	Inner Gondola	Outer Gondola
Aircraft Hours Flown	1,182	1,078
U-boats Entered Zone	40	38
U-boats Sighted	4	14
U-boats Attacked	1	6

Source: Max Schoenfeld, *Stalking the U-boat* (Washington and London: Smithsonian Institute Press, 1995), 46.

A successful attack had to occur within 15–35 seconds after the submarine submerged. Once spotted, surprise was the key to a successful attack that would either damage or destroy a U-boat. Coming out of a cloud bank with the sun behind, the pilot attacked at an angle of 15–45 degrees and flew as low as possible, usually 50–200 feet (15-61m) and dropped a string of depth bombs within 20 feet of the submarine's pressure hull, preset to fall at 50–75ft (15–23m) intervals. On approach and after releasing the bombs, aircraft gunners would fire to suppress the anti-aircraft fire coming from the submarine. During *Gondola*, the 1st Antisubmarine Group flew 111 missions of 1,052 hours during February, sighted 11 U-boats, and attacked eight, with one claimed to have sunk, which was not the case.

On February 10, Lt. William L. Sanford in B-24D named *TIDEWATER LILLIE,* was operating 800 miles off St. Nazaire, at an altitude of 800ft (244m) below a thick cloud bank, when the left waist gunner visually sighted Korvettenkapitän Karl-Ernst Schroeter's U-*752*. The weather was poor, with rough seas, when the crewman saw the submarine's conning disappearing beneath the waves. Yet, approximately 40 percent of the stern protruded out of the water at an angle of some six degrees. The bombardier released six depth bombs; five of the six overshot, but one exploded 30 feet starboard of the vessel. Sanford turned the B-24D

Above: Officers of the 480th inside a burnt-out hanger at an undisclosed location, possibly in England. (AFHRA Reel A4070, 214)

Left: Interrogation of a plane crew from the 480th after a patrol over the Mediterranean. (AFHRA Reel A0522, 550)

to the portside and made a second attack with three depth bombs on the now-awash submarine. One bomb exploded near the port side causing the vessel to lift slightly above the water. A large dome-like air bubble then appeared on the surface, followed by a large pool of oil. Such evidence suggested a probable kill, and Sanford and his crew were given credit for the submarine's destruction. Yet, that was not the case as U-*752* escaped, but a plane from HMS *Archer* sank the U-boat three months later.

The addition of the two AAF antisubmarine squadrons to England immensely aided the fight against U-boats, with 11 attacks occurring between December 1942 and 15 February 1943. During six weeks of operations, the 1st Antisubmarine Group (Provisional) accounted for the mistaken sinking of two submarines, U-*519* and U-*752*, out of 18 sightings. It was not a spectacular outcome, but the arrival

Above left: General Lawson congratulates the crew of *Tidewater Lillie*, s/n 41-23677, of the 2nd Bombing Squadron, 480th Antisubmarine Group, upon sinking a U-boat. (NARA 342-FH-3A09050-23556AC)

Above right: B-24D, s/n 42-40107, named *SUB MISSION* with olive drab and gray or white under surfaces, belonged to the 1st Squadron, Antisubmarine Group. (James Pontolillo)

of the American group did bolster the presence of antisubmarine aircraft, which kept U-boats on the defensive. Air Marshall John Slessor, Air Officer-Commanding in Chief, wrote that the two US squadrons played a central part and incidentally bloodied themselves in antisubmarine warfare. The group honed skills for future operations in which it would account for the destruction of four enemy submarines while operating patrols over the Bay of Biscay and the Mediterranean. Yet, the group paid a price. While operating from the UK, the group lost 71 officers, men, and nine B-24s. Two aircraft were lost crossing the Atlantic; two failed to return from missions, four crashed, and the last was shot down by a German plane in aerial combat.[1]

Known U-boat Encounters by the 1st Antisubmarine Group/ 2037 Antisubmarine Wing November 1942–March 1943

Operations from St. Eval, England

Date	Squadron	U-boat Assessment
December 29	1	Insufficient evidence of damage
December 31	1	No damage assessed
February 6	1	No damage assessed
February 9	1	Insufficient evidence of damage
February 9	2	No damage
February 10	2	No damage assessed
February 10	2	No damage
February 20	1	Probably severely damaged
March 2	1	Insufficient evidence of damage
April 7	1	No damage assessed

Source: Air Force Historical Research Agency (AFHRA) staff at Maxwell AFB, Alabama, Reel A4070, 221–230.

North African Operations (March–November 1943)

On February 10, 1943, the commanding officer of Navy Patrol Squadron 73 (VP-73) sent a letter to the Chief of Naval Operations via the Navy's Commander Fleet Air Wing Fifteen (FAW-15) and the newly appointed Commander Moroccan Sea Force, requesting a change from PBY-5A's to PB4Y's, the Navy's term for B-24s. Because the latter is faster, longer ranged, and more heavily gunned, it was a far better antisubmarine plane. The Commander of Moroccan Sea Forces wired Commander Naval Forces, North West African Waters, who in turn sent a dispatch to the Commander-in-Chief, US Fleet Admiral King, requesting he ask the Chief of Staff, US Army, to make eight Army B-24s available at the earliest possible date. This appeal brought results; on March 9, the first contingent of two Army squadrons, the 1st and 2nd, comprised of the newly established 2037th Antisubmarine Wing, later the 480th Antisubmarine Group, arrived at Port Lyautey for duty under the Commander of FAW-15, Captain G.A. Seitz, USN. On March 9, the first plane carrying Lt. Colonel Roberts arrived at Port Lyautey. Operations began immediately with convoy coverage and antisubmarine patrols per FAW-15's commanding officer, who, as other like-minded naval authorities, saw convoy coverage as the primary mission of patrolling between March and June 1943. In July, Roberts' antisubmarine wing obtained authority to allow an offensive campaign to rid the Mediterranean of enemy submarines.

Coastal Command was sorry to see them go and would have gladly had their help in the intensified bay offensive planned for the spring. However, the US Navy was anxious to have the extra range of B-24 aircraft to protect the approaches to the Mediterranean. By the arrangement of Army and Navy authorities, the squadrons went to Morocco. Coastal Command fully expected the American squadrons would work under its command at Gibraltar. That assumption is shown in letters of Air Marshall Sir John Slessor to Lt. Colonel Roberts between March and May 1943, "I know the RAF at Gibraltar will soon experience the same cheerful and efficient cooperation that you have shown us in Cornwall…I wish you had not left St. Eval–we have had some real good hunting in the last few weeks and are really killing U-boats".[2]

The ground echelon of the 2037th Antisubmarine Wing (redesignated 480th Antisubmarine Group) arrived in French Morocco in March 1943. (AFHRA Reel B0638, 348)

Craw Field, French Morocco, where the 480th Antisubmarine Group operated between March and November 1943. (AFHRA Reel A0522, 548)

Varga Girl Virgin, s/n 41-24196, of the 480th Antisubmarine Group, 2nd Squadron, piloted by Zenon "Sy" Sykuta. (Mike Fitzpatrick)

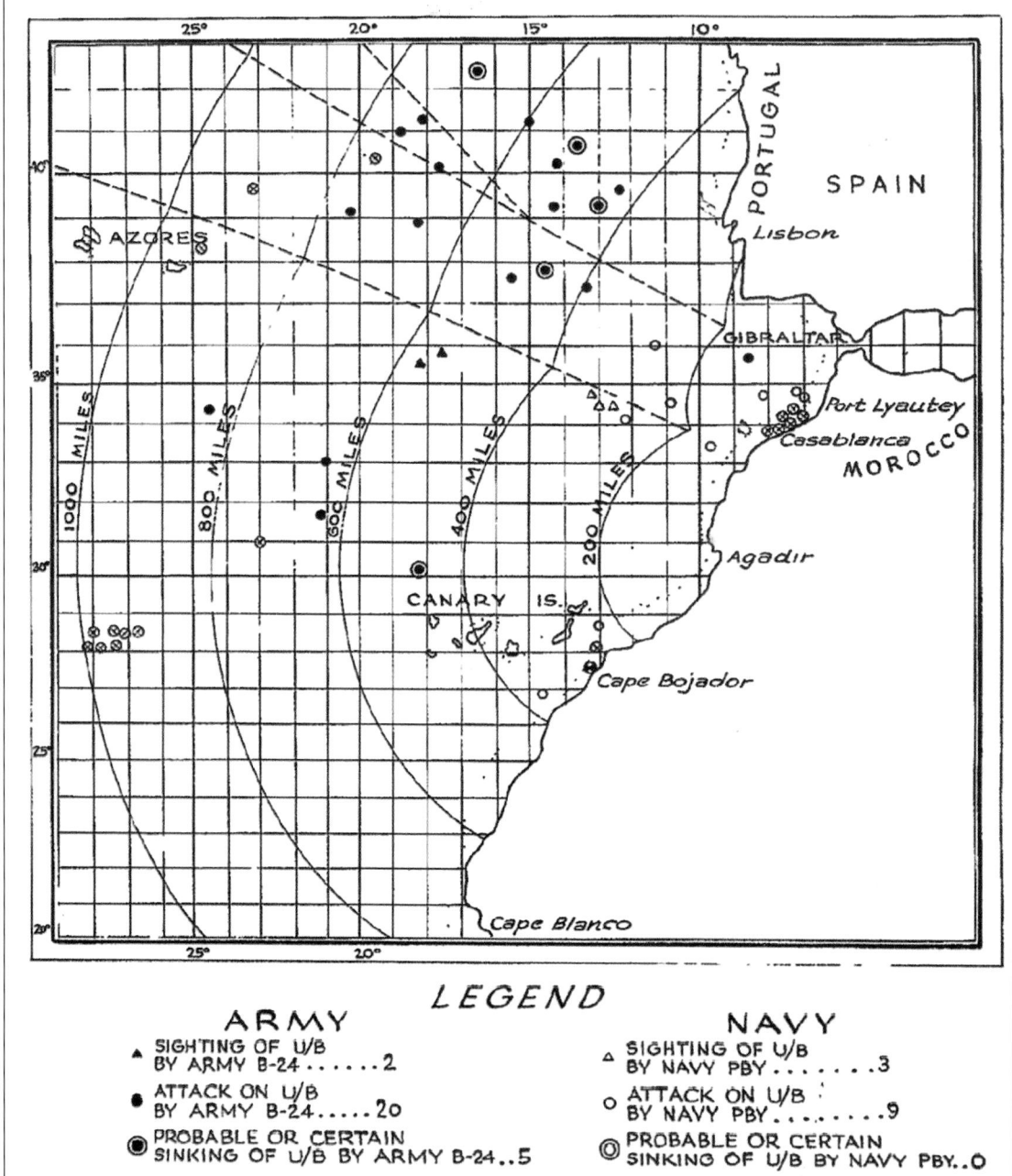

A map showing the Moroccan Sea Frontier of attacks made by Army and Navy planes from November 11, 1942, to July 15, 1943. (AFHRA A4070, 349)

The enlisted tent quarters for personnel of the 480th at Naval Air Station, Port Lyautey. (AFHRA Reel A0522, 550)

The arrival of long-range B-24Ds vindicated the planners at Port Lyautey, who expressed the need for VLR aircraft as the shorter-range PBY-5A lacked the necessary range as the B-24 that could frequently cover areas where submarines were known to patrol. The ASW missions were named *Killer Sweep*, *Madeira Sweep*, and *Canary Sweep*. Those areas were beyond the range of naval aircraft staging from Port Lyautey at the time but not of the B-24s. Yet, U-boat hunting was not initially the primary duty of the two Army Liberator squadrons upon arrival to the displeasure of the group's commanding officer. Roberts was not happy providing convoy coverage instead of hunting enemy submarines. The commanding officer saw it as a waste of his unit, which he thought would be better utilized for operations in the Bay of Biscay. However, the Navy insisted upon the integrity of the Moroccan Sea Frontier as its operational preserve, both for air and surface forces. The Commander, Naval Authorities in North African waters (COMNAVNAW), insisted that the control of the frontier was a Navy responsibility and would control Army and Navy units assigned to it. He sent a radiogram to COMINCH on April 18 in which he wrote:

> My position has been and will continue to be that the control of the Moroccan Sea Frontier is a US Naval responsibility…that its primary mission is the protection of convoys from [the] US and secondarily that of other convoys passing through the area; that the employment of the B-24s, which were initially requested by [the] US Navy is necessary to extend and augment the coverage which can be provided by the Navy planes.[3]

Lt. Colonel Roberts called General Larson's attention on June 7, 1943, to the unprofitable use of his VLR planes, and claimed his squadron would be better suited in the Atlantic. He thought his crews were the most able antisubmarine personnel in the AAF and required them in the Bay of Biscay Campaign and not in the Mediterranean, where there were relatively few targets. He believed every officer and man would gladly return to St. Eval, where they saw real concrete accomplishment. He wrote on June 7 to General Larson: "We wonder if we are being used to [the] best advantage by operating here…we are being employed where there is a relatively small number of targets. We read weekly the numerous attacks by Coastal Command in the Bay and the Atlantic; we are confident that we could be more effective there than they are"[4].

Above left: A B-24D, s/n 41-24261, named *TIGER Lil* and its crew belong to the 2nd Squadron. (AFHRA Reel B0638, 393)

Above right: DEE WABBIT, no s/n, appears to have served with the 480th Antisubmarine Group. (James Pontolillo)

In another letter to General Larson, he wrote, "I simply raise the question and do not mean to imply that I know the answer because there are many considerations of which I am unaware"[5].

By this time, the 1st and 2nd squadrons were operating under the designation 480th Antisubmarine Group. Their presence aided in keeping U-boats on the defensive. Yet, a disgruntled Roberts asked how many ships would have been sunk in the Bay of Biscay if the group had not been in North Africa; the group would have sunk more submarines if it had stayed covering the Bay of Biscay. Coastal Command would lack the presence of an American B-24 group from late March to July 1943 when the 479th Antisubmarine Group arrived at St. Eval. Meanwhile, until July, the entire Army outfit at Port Lyautey felt left out of the big hunt in the bay. However, statistics show the group spent more time in antisubmarine sweeps than convoy coverage, but what would have been the outcome if it had been given additional time for submarine hunting? The statistics for the 480th Antisubmarine Group conducting antisubmarine sweeps and convoy coverage during 1943 are shown in the following table:

480th Group Antisubmarine and Convoy Coverage

Month	Antisubmarine Sweep	Convoy Coverage	Total Hours Flown
March	400	–	400
April	1,122	397	1,519
May	674	733	1,407
June	1,119	541	1,660
July	1,544	624	2,163
August	883	795	1,678

Source: *The Antisubmarine Command, U.S. Air Force Historical Study No. 107* (short title *AAFRH-7*), 123.

In the coming months, the 2037th Wing/480th Group made roughly ten times as many sightings per hour of flying time as the Navy PBY Catalinas operating simultaneously, primarily due to the B-24's extended range. Of all sightings by Roberts' group between March and July 1943, more than 20 percent resulted in attacks on U-boats, and 10 percent resulted in kills. The record was primarily due to sound tactics employed by the pilot and visual or radar sightings by the crew.

Antisubmarine Sweeps

Operations began out of Craw Field, Port Lyautey, and, not long afterward, a fully surfaced U-boat was sighted and attacked between the Azore Islands and Madeiras, Spain, by the crew of First Lt. Sanford. On 22 March, Sanford's plane *TIDEWATER TILLIE* spotted U-*524* while the aircraft flew leisurely at 200ft (70m) coming in and out of the cloud bank. The co-pilot spotted the submarine, and Sanford made a 90-degree turn while losing altitude. The plane was not detected as the U-boat continued on a straight course while surfaced. At 200ft (70m) altitude, the bombardier released four depth bombs that enveloped the vessel. U-*524* settled by the stern with the conning tower projecting out of the water. Several of the B-24's crew members saw men clinging to debris, yet none of the 52-man crew survived. Four months would pass before the group conducted additional successes against enemy submarines. After the March 22 success by Lt. Sanford, there was an impasse on whether to allow the Army B-24 squadrons to take the offensive against U-boats – a drought ensued that would remain until July 1943.

The presence of U-boats in the Mediterrananean never was that significant in all of 1943, 13 making the trip during that year. Additionally, a the Mediterranean and the waters approaching it were dangerous due to the large presence of Allied ships and aircraft. The small number of U-boats and extreme cautiousness that deterred U-boat commanders from making their former liberal use of the radio for transmitting messages to Berlin may also account for the 2037th Antisubmarine Wing inability conduct a single successful attack for months. However, U-boats did manage to sink 86 merchant vessels and damage 18 warships during the year. In early April a U-boat torpedoed and sank two merchant vessels in a convoy south of the Azores. Wing dispatched B-24s to that general area on April 7 and there discovered a surfaced enemy submarine. Terrific anti-aircraft fire and skillful maneuvering enabled the U-boat to submerge safely. Afterward, the sinking of a 3,000-ton merchant vessel led the 2037th to undertake sweeps off the Canary and Madeira islands.

June was a month of almost breathless calm as U-boats continued clearly on the defensive. Only three U-boats, on average, were estimated to be within the Moroccan Sea Frontier. At the same time, the main concentration of German submarines located in the Eastern Atlantic shifted to an area south-west of the Azores. There, they waited for African-bound convoys.

The position of guarding convoys relaxed between July 6 and 14 when the Allied invasion of Sicily commenced. The 2037th Antisubmarine Wing was renamed the 480th Antisubmarine Group, and began cooperating with the RAF at Gibraltar, conducting antisubmarine (A/S) sweeps. Conversely,

Above left: A depth charge explodes along the U-*524*s, nearly missing the submarine. (AFHRA Reel C0 174, 1097)

Above right: U-*524* is under attack by Lieutenant Sandford. The depth charge appears to be approximately 200ft beyond the submarine. (AFHRA Reel C0174, 1098)

Above left: A depth charge explodes with the bow and conning tower of U-*524* clearly shown as the U-boat attempts to crash dive. (AFHRA Reel B0638, 883)

Above right: A devastating explosion from a depth charge rocks U-*524*. The conning tower can be seen on the left. (AFHRA Reel CO 174, 1121)

Above left: Behind the B-24D, bubbling water, oil, and debris mark the end of U-*524*. Only six of the 54-man crew survived. (AFHRA Reel C0174, 1119)

Above right: Survivors from U-*524*. One group hangs on to a cylindrical object while the other clings to a life raft. (AFHRA Reel B0638, 882)

(Dönitz) ordered U-boats in July 1943 to attack shipping in the waters of the Iberian Peninsula, the Mediterranean, and those heading towards the United Kingdom under the wolfpack named Geir 1 to 3. The 480th Antisubmarine Wing was tagged to protect convoys and attack U-boats in the area if the occasion presented itself.

July proved to be the month in which the group excelled in antisubmarine sweeps–on the 7th, 1st Squadron's Lieutenant T.A. Isley seriously damaged a U-boat 230 miles south-west of Lisbon. First Squadron's, B-24 codename "K," flown by Lieutenant Walter S. McDonnell, intercepted Type VIIC U-*951* on its first patrol while operating with Wolfpack Geir 2 and under the command of 32-year-old Oberleutnant Kurt Pressel. The plane's radar picked up the vessel seven miles north-west of Cape St. Vincent, Portugal. The pilot visually sighted the surfaced submarine from five miles away and dived down until the Liberator was just 50ft (15m) above the water.

The plane took several hits from accurate flak, with one 20mm shell bursting in the nose area, wounding the navigator 1st Lt. John E. Richards, bombardier 2nd Lt. James R. Goosby, co-pilot 2nd Lt. Wilfred N. Lind, and assistant radio operator Sargeant Robert Just. The bombardier, although wounded, managed to release seven depth bombs that straddled the submarine. Immediately, it appeared U-*951* broke in two aft

Above left: U-*951* is under attack by Lieutenant Walter McDonnell of the 1st Antisubmarine Squadron on July 7, 1943. The depth bomb fell short by at least 200ft. (AFHRA Reel A4073, 1659)

Above right: U-*951*'s bow is shown on the left as a depth bomb explodes close to the vessel, probably causing severe damage. (AFHRA Reel A4073, 1661)

of the conning tower, and all 46 crew members aboard perished. Aboard McDonnell's plane, Richards and Goosby went to the flight deck to receive first aid. The navigator received a chest wound, and the bombardier sustained a severe gash in the arm, and both were bleeding profusely from multiple flesh wounds inflicted by flying glass and pieces of shrapnel. McDonnell flew back to the base, where an ambulance transported them to the hospital where Goosby, Lind, and Just had recovered. This encounter, as one Air Force historian said at the time, was a textbook example of how crews performed their duties well:

> Group records stated an attack succeeds only when a crew functions as a team and each member retains its resourcefulness and initiative. Many factors are considered, all in a minute or even less. Hence the long hours of training and the seemingly endless days of instruction the officers and men received. The kill involved all phases of U-boat combat and how each crew member discharged his duties.[6]

Two days later, flying at 3,200ft (975m) on July 9, 1943, Lt. W.S. Gerhardt, the bombardier of a B-24D from the 1st Squadron, spotted Korvettenkapitän Siegfried Strelow's Type VIIC U-*435* west of Lisbon. The veteran of eight patrols, 13 ships were sunk by the submarine, but this time, while operating with Wolfpack Geir 2, U-*435* would not survive. The pilot of the Liberator, Lt. T.E. Kuenning, saw the submarine and immediately put the plane into a dive, leveling off at 50ft (15m). Gerhardt released a train of six depth bombs straggling the submarine's bow section just aft of the conning tower. The Liberator's pilot swung the bomber around for a second attack in which the bombardier released two more depth bombs on the still-surfaced U-boat. The explosives detonated aft of the conning tower, and the bomber's crew saw the bow rise 15ft (4.6m) out of the water, followed by the hull sinking stern first; the entire crew perished. A British Wellington of 179 Squadron was previously credited for U-*435*'s fate.

Left: U-*951* suffered from a series of depth charge attacks from McDonnel's B-24D. In this photograph, one fell to the port side while another exploded close to the vessel's starboard. (AFHRA Reel A4073, 1550)

Below left: A pair of depth charges on the port and starboard sides of U-*951* have exploded in front of the U-boat's deck gun. (AFHRA Reel A4073, 1553)

Below right: Another depth charge attack envelops U-*951* forward of the conning tower, probably causing it to sink. The entire crew of 46 men perished. (AFHRA Reel A4052, 1552)

Radar once again played an important role when Kapitänleutnant Erich Würdemann's Type IXC U-*506*, a combat veteran with 14 ships sunk to its credit, was spotted on radar 20 miles north-west of Lisbon, on July 12, by a B-24D, flown by Lt. Ernst Salm. U-*506* is known for picking up 151 survivors of the ship *Laconia* when Lt. James Harden of the 343rd Bombardment Squadron piloting a B-24 attacked the U-boat on September 17, 1942, forcing the boat to dive, leaving survivors in the water. Ten months later, on July 12, 1943, pilot Lt. Salm of the 1st Squadron spotted the submarine at 200ft (61m) and broke through the solid overcast to engage the surfaced U-*506*.

The submarine was just a mile away on the starboard side; none of the vessel's personnel were observed topside as the Liberator's bombardier dropped seven depth bombs. The crew saw the explosions straddle the submarine, and as the pilot made a verticle turn at 100ft (30m) the U-boat broke in two. Oil and large air bubbles appeared for several minutes as Salm circled the area at 100ft (30m). Crew members aboard the plane watched the survivors in the water. Salm recalled, "They seemed to be watching us. Maybe they thought

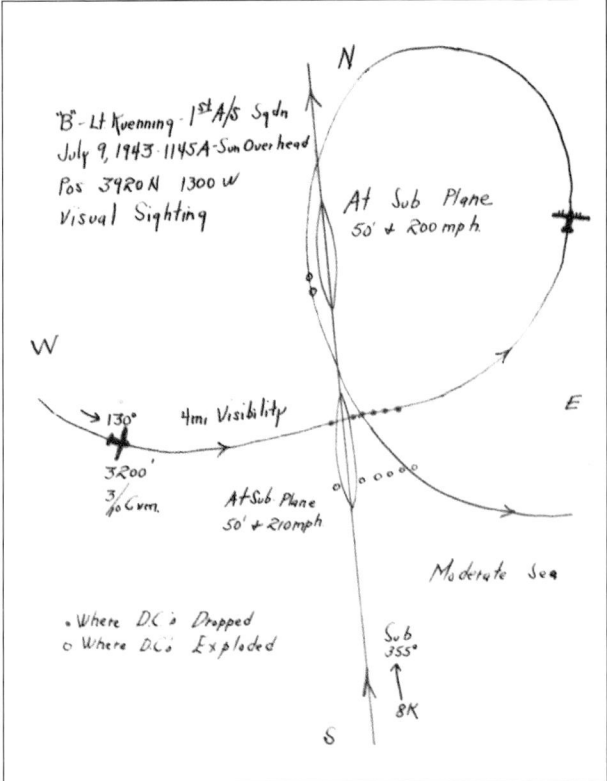

Right: The attack against U-*435* on July 9 by Lieutenant W.W. Kuenning of 1st Squadron, 480th Antisubmarine Group, is shown in the after-action report. U-*435* sank nine ships under the leadership of Korvettenkapitän Siegfried Strelow. The entire crew of 48 men perished. (AFHRA Reel A4073, 1619)

Below: U-*506* was spotted on July 9, 1943, by a B-24D piloted by Lieutenant Ernst Salm of 1st Squadron, 480th Antisubmarine Group. The submarine had sunk or damaged 15 ships before being destroyed. (AFHRA Reel B0638, 353)

Above left: U-*524* is enveloped by water from exploding depth charges released by Lieutenant Salm's plane. (AFHRA, Reel 0638, 3522)

Above right: Depth bombs from the B-24 explode, straddling U-*506* off Lisbon, Portugal, on July 9, 1943. (AFHRA Reel B0638, 885)

Left: Oil-covered survivors of U-*506* can be seen at the top left after Lieutenant Salm's attack. Only six of the 54-man view survived. (AFHRA Reel BO638, 886)

Below: Lieutenant Ernst Salm and his crew 480th, which sank U-*506*. (AFHRA Reel A0522, 550)

we would give them the same treatment they would have given us…but they seemed to have fear on their faces."⁷ Fifteen survivors were counted in the water as a life raft was dropped down to them, as well as life vests and K rations. Six of the U-*506*'s crew would survive out of the 54-man crew after being rescued by a British destroyer.

During nine days in July 1943, the group conducted 12 antisubmarine attacks, with four submarines sunk and, despite heavy convoy traffic, not one merchant vessel fell to a U-boat in the areas covered by group aircraft as U-boats began retiring from the waters of the Iberian Peninsula. In 20 attacks conducted through August, no further encounters with U-boats materialized after July 14, but convoy coverage continued. It became clear that the battered and broken remains of Dönitz's once proud U-boat flotilla in the Gibraltar–Morocco area had limped northward to the security of ports in France. Antisubmarine sweeps continued unsuccessfully; however, by this time, the group began encountering enemy aircraft that would last through October 1943.

In September, ten B-24s and their crew of the 1st Antisubmarine Squadron were deployed to Protville, Tunisia, a base 35 miles north-west of Tunis, operating under the Northwest African Coastal Air Force. Conditions were lackluster, with personnel having to live in small tents. Here, they provided antisubmarine sweeps between Sicily and Naples. The 480th Group's overall casualty rate was near 50 percent during operations in England and North Africa. The 480th Antisubmarine Group continued operations until November 1943, when Navy B-24s arrived. The successful operations of the 480th Antisubmarine groups did not come out without loss of life and aircraft. In total, 30 officers and men lost their lives while based in Morocco, and seven bombers were lost – of these, two failed to return from a mission, two crashed, and one was shot down in aerial combat. VB-111, equipped with B-24s, the PB4Y-1, as the Navy called the bomber, arrived at Port Lyautey in October. FAW-15 took over all convoy and antisubmarine operations, while the 480th left Morocco in November, returning to Langley Field for demobilization. Upon hearing about Navy squadrons replacing the 480th Antisubmarine Group, Air Marshall Slessor wrote to Lt. Colonel Roberts that the policy made little sense; his opinion went unheeded.

The camp scene for the 480th Antisubmarine Group at Protville, Tunisia, where elements of the 480th were temporarily based. (AFHRA Reel A0-522, 551)

The 480th Antisubmarine Group, March–July 1943

Operations From French Morocco

Date	Squadron	U-boat Assessment
22 March	2	Sunk
7 April	1	No damage
7 April	1	No damage assessed
7 May	2	Probably slightly damaged
7 May	2	Insufficient damage assessed
15 May	2	Probably slightly damaged
3 June	1	No damage
19 June	2	Probably slightly damaged
6 July	1	No damage assessed
7 July	1	Probably severely damaged
7 July	1	Sunk
8 July	2	Probably severe damage
9 July	1	Sunk
9 July	2	Probably slightly damaged
9 July	1	No damage assessed
10 July	2	No damage assessed
11 July	1	Insufficient evidence assessed
12 July	1	Sunk
13 July	2	Insufficient damage assessed
14 July	2	Probably slightly damaged

Source: Air Force Historical Research Agency (AFHRA) staff at Maxwell AFB, Alabama, Reel A4070, 221–230.

A fatal accident of a B-24D (M) that occurred in September 1943. The entire crew of 10 were killed. (AFHRA Reel B0638, 375)

The mission of the 1st and 2nd Antisubmarine Squadrons was a period of pioneering. Officers and men of the two squadrons met severe operational problems and overcame them. Quarters were inadequate, operating facilities were primitive, and the weather in England during the winter was miserable. The operations under 19 Coastal Command proved quite compatible, but at Port Lyautey, under Navy control, such a relationship was strained. Yet, the USAAF group conducted 30 attacks against U-boats around England and French Morrocco, resulting in four sinkings. Their presence reduced the effectiveness of U-boats operating in the Bay of Biscay and the waters of the Mediterranean.

A graveside memorial for a crew killed from the 480th Antisubmarine Group during operations in North Africa. (AFHRA Reel A0522 547)

Chapter 6
The 479th Antisubmarine Group

In June 1943, a pair of USAAF B-24 squadrons, the 4th and 19th, participated in Bay of Biscay antisubmarine operations; those two units would become the backbone for establishing the 479th Antisubmarine Group. This group became the second and last USAAF Antisubmarine force to operate from the UK. Moving the 1st Antisubmarine Group to Morrocco left a three-month gap in AAF coverage of the North Sea and the Bay of Biscay. Fog and rain caused the cancellation of effective air operations until July 13, when a joint British-American task force of VLR aircraft began offensive actions against U-boats in the Bay of Biscay. This task force deployed in two antisubmarine areas in the bay known as "Musketry" and "Seaslug." The first of two squadrons, the 4th and 19th, began arriving at St. Eval, England on June 30, 1943 in what would become the 479th Antisubmarine Group; ultimately, the group would consist of four antisubmarine squadrons – the 4th, 6th, 19th, and 22nd Antisubmarine Squadrons with the latter two arriving in August.

Aerial photograph of St. Eval, England, where the 480th Antisubmarine Group was based between November 1942 and March 1943 and by the 479th Antisubmarine Group from July to September 1943. (James Pontodillo)

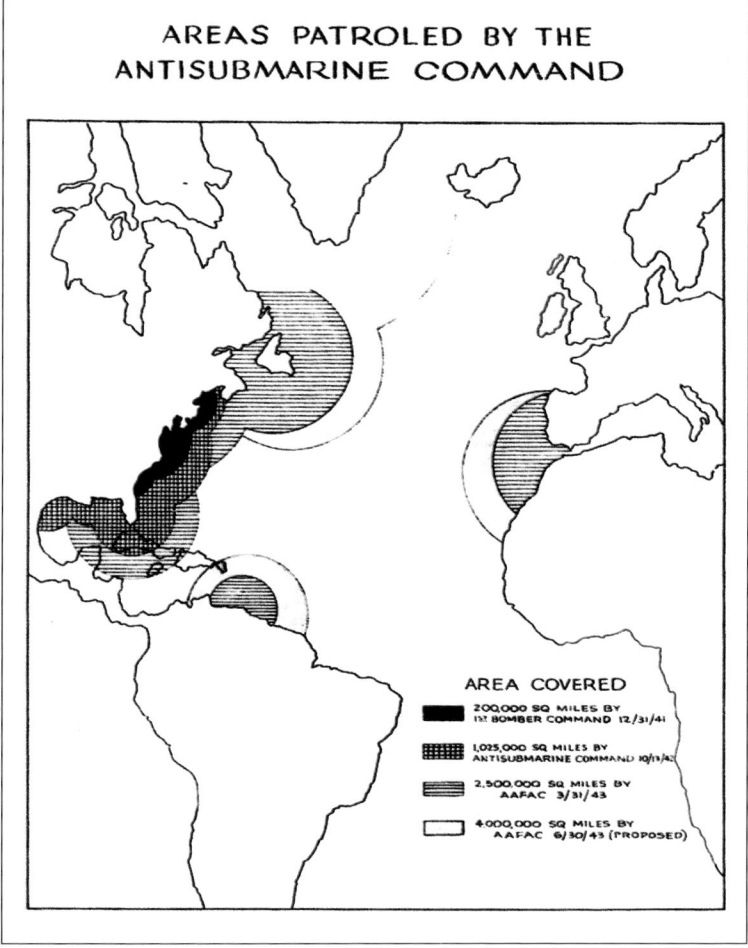

A map showing antisubmarine activities by Army aircraft between 1941 and 1943. (AFHRA Reel 4058, 53)

On July 13, 1943, the group flew its first operation as an active part in the Musketry campaign. During that time, a U-boat's anti-aircraft defenses probably shot down a B-24 from the Group. During 19 days from July 13 to August 2, 479th B-24s from the 4th and 19th Antisubmarine Squadron's sighted 12 submarines and attacked seven – three were sunk: U-558, U-404, and U-706. During July, the 479th Antisubmarine Group conducted 26 percent of all attacks in the Bay of Biscay. Still, the month proved to be the high-water mark as the group conducted 29 attacks that month compared to seven in August. However, the concentration of U-boats remained relatively unchanged, with 10–20 U-boats sighted during August.

U-boat Attacks by the 479th Antisubmarine Group

On July 20, U-558 commanded by 28-year-old Kapitänleutnant Günther Krech, fell victim to Charles F. Gallmeir of 19th Antisubmarine Squadron and a British Halifax of 58 Squadron when caught north-west of Cape Ortegal, Spain. Previously, Krech sank 19 ships between August 28, 1941, and February 23, 1942; U-558 finished its patrol and was heading back to port when a British Wellington of 179 Squadron spotted it on July 15, but thick flak drove off the plane. Two days later, an RAF Coastal Command B-24 attacked, but it, too, was driven off. On the 20th, the submarine's anti-aircraft fire shot down a 19th Squadron B-24 piloted by 1st Lt. Harold Dyment; there were no survivors. However, U-558's luck ran out that same day.

U-558's captain decided to surface to recharge the vessel's batteries, feeling safe from air or surface attack from the enemy due to poor visibility. However, the submarine's deck watch was surprised when 19th Squadron's 1st Lt. Gallmeir's B-24 suddenly appeared. The alarm sounded, and an effort to start the diesel engines began, but the motors would not immediately function. The plane's bombardier dropped four depth bombs, with one landing approximately 50ft off the port bow. Flak from U-558's 20mm guns became heavy as the B-24 passed over, causing the plane to be hit in several locations and wounding the left waist gunner. The Liberator released a stick of seven depth charges set at 25 feet. The U-boat had again altered course to starboard, and the stick of depth charges exploded along the U-boat's portside at an estimated angle of 170 degrees. The charges crippled the U-boat, and it could no longer dive; soon, water entered the battery compartment, and chlorine gas built up, causing the deaths of many of the ship's personnel. However, Gallmeir's B-24 took a hit on the port engine, and the left waist gunner was wounded in both legs, forcing a return to base.

The British Halifax from 58 Squadron bomber appeared and, passing over the target, straddled it with eight 250lb bombs while machine gunning those on the submarine's deck. The U-boat keeled over on its port beam, and the bow emerged suddenly from the water before being obscured by the spray of the exploding depth charges. Knowing their boat was doomed, approximately 20 men climbed on to the forward deck only to have the British aircraft fire on them, and several fell into the water. The U-boat settled rapidly by the stern, fire from the boat having ceased. About 40 bodies and those who survived the sinking spread over an area of a 1/4 mile square. During that day, most of the survivors, including Krech,

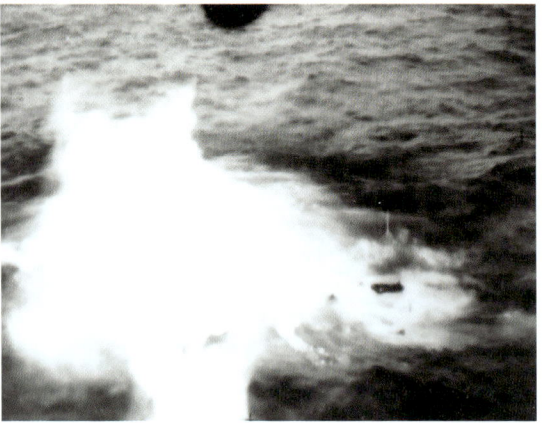

Above left: U-558 fell victim to Charles F. Gallmeir of the 19th Squadron of the 479- Group and a British Halifax of 58 Squadron. A crewman aboard the Halifax took a photograph showing the attack on U-558. A depth charge has just exploded near the submarine. (AFHRA Reel B0637, 1317)

Above right: U-558 looks like it is split into two from a depth charge, with the bow and stern barely visible. The U-boat sank or damaged 21 ships during its career. (AFHRA Reel B0637, 1812)

Left: The bow of U-558 can be seen (center left) rising out of the water, while the stern is on the center-right. (AFHRA Reel B0637, 1811)

hung on to the dinghy, but most disappeared or died, most to exposure to the gas. On the following day, there were only eight men left. On July 23, there were six, and one of the six died from drinking seawater. The five survivors soon recovered a canister of fresh water dropped by a British Liberator. On July 24, a Canadian destroyer rescued them.

A week later, on July 28, Major Stephen D. McElroy of the 4th Squadron spotted a surfaced U-404 and proceeded to attack. The submarine's new captain, 24-year-old Oberleutnant Adolf Schönberg, assumed command on July 20 and sailed from St Nazaire on the 24th. Four days out of port, U-404 had encountered a B-24 from the 4th Squadron flown by Major Stephen McElroy. Depth charges hung up during the first run, enabling the U-boat to crash-dive. The plane's pilot decided to wait for the boat to resurface, which lasted four hours. Upon visual sighting, McElroy flew down the U-boat's track, and the bombardier released several depth charges. At the same time, the B-24's gunners attempted to suppress anti-aircraft fire. The depth bombs exploded, causing a large oil patch to appear along with debris. However, intense anti-aircraft fire damaged the aircraft's radio and to the instruments of number three and four engines, forcing a return to base, but not before sending a contact message.

First Lt. Arthur J. Hammer of the 4th Antisubmarine Squadron set a course back to the base as his plane flew 150 miles north of Cape Finisterre after an uneventful flight when the surfaced U-404 came into view. He changed course to come out of the sun, but the boat's gunners spotted him and

Right: Debris from U-*558* and crew members aboard a life raft (center left). Kapitänleutnant Günther Krech, the submarine's commanding officer, and four other men survived. (AFHRA Reel B0637, 1815)

Below: Lieutenant Gallmeir and other members of the 479th Antisubmarine Group are wearing the awards they received during a ceremony at an air base in St. Eval, England. (NARA 342-FH-3A07381-76504AC)

began putting up heavy flak. Hammer continued his run while his top turret and nose guns opened fire. The Liberator's bombardier released eight depth bombs, all straddling the enemy submarine. Hammer swung around for a second run, with three of four depth bombs falling short and one that fell 5ft (2m) from the hull. The German flak gunners were becoming accurate as rounds knocked out the No. 1 engine.

Meanwhile, the nose gunner ran out of ammunition, and the top turret guns became jammed. Defenseless, he called off another attack as a Coastal Command Liberator of 224 Squadron arrived. Seven more depth bombs fell out of the British bomber, straddling the submarine, with one falling alongside the conning tower. The submarine disappeared under the waves, resurfaced, and then submerged again with the bow projecting high above the water. The second Liberator made a second depth bomb attack, and the U-boat disappeared. Two extensive oil patches and two large air bubbles appeared, along with ten men with life jackets, yet none of U-404's 51 crew members survived.

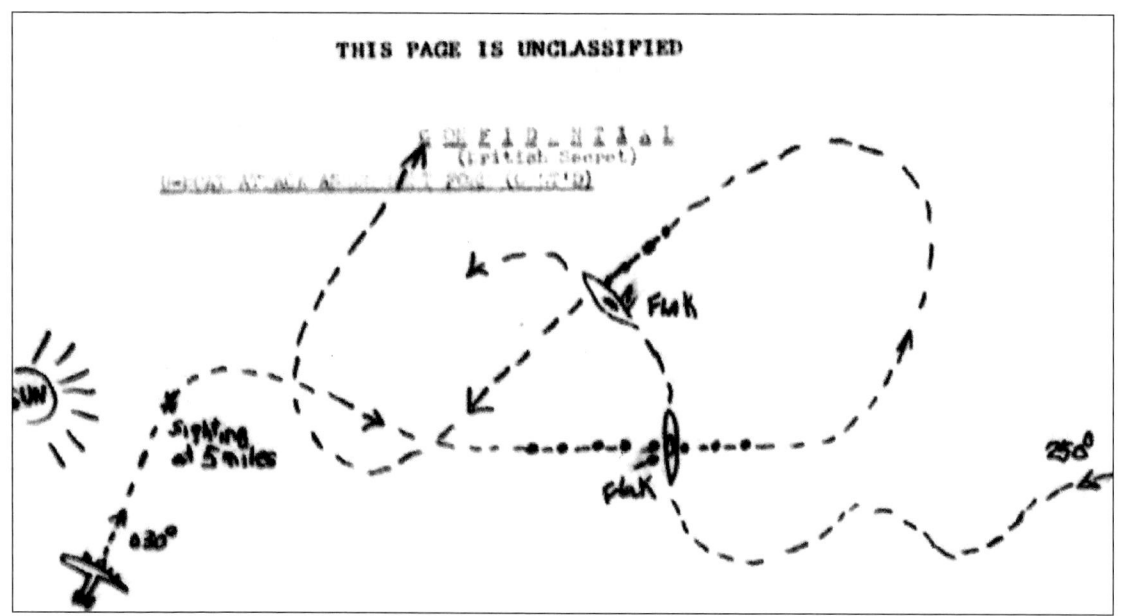

Above: An after-action illustration prepared by Lieutenant Arthur J. Hamilton shows the track of the B-24D as it attacked U-*404*. (AFHRA Reel A4073, 1787)

Left: Air bubbles appear on the surface where the U-*404* went down, indicating air loss inside the U-boat. The submarine had previously sunk or damaged 17 ships. (AFHRA Reel B0637, 1818)

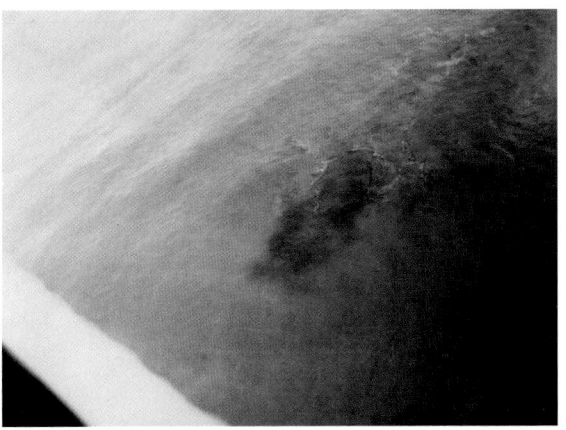

Above left: The appearance of a round pool of oil is indicative that U-*404* has been severely or mortally damaged. (AFHRA Reel B0637, 2820)

Above right: A larger pool of oil appears on the surface, indicating the loss of U-*404*. The entire crew of 51 men perished. (AFHRA Reel B0637, 1819)

On August 2, a B-24D flown by Captain Joseph L Hamilton of the 4th Antisubmarine Squadron picked up on the radar U-*706*, north-west of Cape Ortegal, Spain, while flying at 2,500ft (762m). The target, commanded by 27-year-old Korvettenkapitän Alexander von Zitzewitz, was 20 miles away and had been unsuccessfully attacked by a British Hamden of 415 Squadron earlier. Machine gun fire from the Liberator killed U-*706*'s captain as the bombardier released a train of 12 depth charges from 50ft (15m)

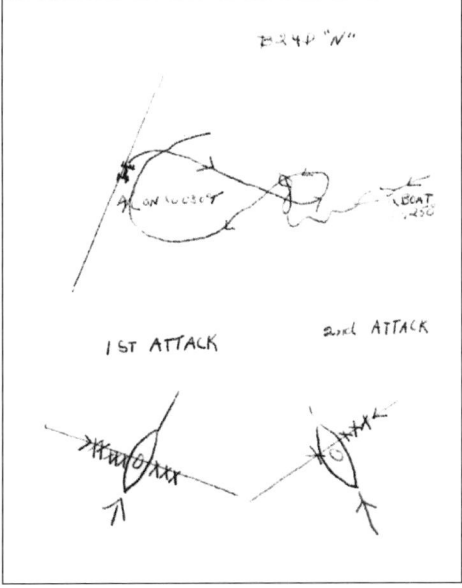

Above left: Strafing and what appears to be a depth charge released against U-*706* by Lieutenant Joseph L Hammer on August 2, 1943. (AFHRA Reel B0637, 1818)

Above right: Illustration of the after-action report detailing the attack on U-*706* by Lieutenant Hammer's crew. (AFHRA Reels BO 637, 1640)

above. The explosives straddled the submarine, causing it to sink stern first, and disappearing in ten seconds. Among the oil debris were 15 survivors. The plane dropped a dingy, and five men climbed aboard. Four would survive out of the 46-man crew.

The 479th Antisubmarine Group sighted and attacked eight German submarines in three months of active operations from July to August, resulting in three sinkings. The group doubled in size between July and August 1943 as squadrons 6 and 22 arrived from Gander, Newfoundland, thus forming the 479th Antisubmarine Group under the command of Lt. Colonel Howard Moore. The addition of

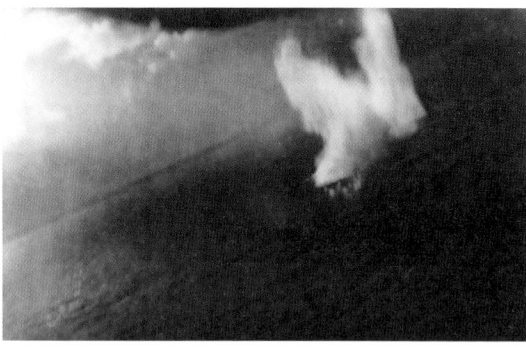

Top left: U-*706* is under attack by a B-24D flown by Lieutenant Hammer of the 4th Squadron. The U-boat was spotted on August 2, 1943, northwest of Cape Ortegal, Spain. Note the explosion from a depth charge has fallen long. (AFHRA Reel B0637, 2018)

Top right: A plume of water from an exploding depth charge attack against U-*706*. The bow can be seen in the left-center section of the photograph. (AFHRA Reel B0637, 1831)

Above left, above right and left: An explosion by a depth charge near U-*706* from Lt. Hammer. The explosive fell some 100–200ft long. The submarine sank, leaving four survivors of the 46 crew members. (NARA 342-FH-3A26479-A76647AC)

Above: Lieutenant Young and crew were part of the 4th Antisubmarine Squadron crew with B-24D s/n 42-40962 at St. Eval, England, in 1943. Note the 15 bomb markings showing the number of depth charge attacks. (NARA 342-FH-3A11895-76490AC)

Right: Lieutenant Dustin and crew of the 4th or 19th Antisubmarine Squadron, 479th Antisubmarine Group, pose beside the B-24D named JUG HAID, s/n 42-40362. (NARA 342-FH-3A11898-76495AC)

24 aircraft from the arrival of two squadrons created packed conditions at St. Eval, forcing the 6th and 9th Squadrons to base at Dunkswell in Devon, which began flying missions in late August. The last engagement by a group plane occurred when 1st Lt. J.O. Bolin unsuccessfully attacked an unidentified U-boat on September 7, 1943. By November, the 479th Antisubmarine Group had disbanded, and Navy squadrons of Fleet Air Wing 7 (FAW-7) took control of the antisubmarine effort. The Group lost five aircraft and 37 personnel between July and September 1943.

Above: Lieutenant Frank Perdue and crew belonging to the 19th Antisubmarine Squadron are standing beside their B-24 *BISCAY BELLE* at St. Eval, England. The aircraft is a later model displaying the nose turret. The 4th and 19th squadrons initially formed the 479th group. (NARE 342-FH-3A11896-76491AC)

Left: The 479th Antisubmarine Group's B-24D *THE BLIND BAT*, s/n 42-40750. The AN/ARN glide scope antenna is on the left, and on the top center is the RC-103 antenna. (342-FH-3A12724-73930AC)

Known U-boat Encounters by the 479th Antisubmarine Group

Date	Squadron	Assessment
18 July	4	Insufficient evidence of damage
20 July	19	Sunk
20 July	19	Probably severely damage
28 July	4	Probably severely damage
28 July	4	Sunk
30 July	19	No damage
2 August	4	Sunk
7 September	19	None

* One unaccounted date*

Source: *The Antisubmarine Command, U.S. Air Force Historical Study No. 107.*

Captain Pop Owens (center) and his crew of the 479th Antisubmarine Group in the reading room at St. Eval, England, before or after conducting an antisubmarine patrol. (NARA 342-FH-3A14717-76492AC)

Combat Crew Members of the 22nd Squadron, 479th Antisubmarine Group, take time out for a game of cards at St. Eval, England. The squadron arrived in August 1943. (NARA 342-FH-3A14718-76494AC)

Chapter 7
Encounters with German Aircraft

The 479th and 480th Antisubmarine Groups encountered enemy aircraft while operating in England and French Morrocco beginning in February 1943 and lasting through October 1943. Crews were told not to engage enemy planes whenever possible. Still, enemy aircraft would attack lone B-24s patrolling over the English Channel and the Bay of Biscay. The mission assigned to AAF Antisubmarine did not mention combat with enemy aircraft. Still, there is some truth in the cynical remark of a young pilot of the 480th Group at Port Lyautey in September 1943 when he said, "We are not hunting U-boats anymore. We are hunting Focke Wolfe 200s."[1]

The 2037 Antisubmarine Group (480th) encountered or observed enemy planes between December 1942 and February 1943 while based at St. Eval. First Lieutenant W.S. Johnson of the 1st Squadron and his crew encountered enemy aircraft on three separate dates, with his plane sustaining damage during one engagement. The only loss of an airplane by the group while based in England occurred on February 26, 1943, when B-24D, serial number 41-23820, piloted by 1st Lieutenant C.A. Tomlinson of 1st Squadron, when a Ju-88, a twin-engine fighter, flown by Oberleutnant Stolle of squadron 8/JG2 caught and shot down the B-24 75 miles north-west of Brest, France. A patrolling aircraft spotted a pair of empty life rafts from Tomlinson's B-24. Those in the 479th Antisubmarine Group encountered primarily Junker Ju-88s throughout operations from July 26 to October 17–the 479th lost two B-24s to German aircraft between August 8 and September 8, 1943. On August 8, B-24D 42-40555, codenamed Q, piloted by 4th Antisubmarine Squadron Captain Reuben Thomas encountered five Ju-88s and, in a running battle, was shot down by Hauptmann Horst Grahl of squadron V/KG 40 with the loss of the entire crew.

Pilot Lieutenant Charlie Moore, with check-pilot 1st Lieutenant Silas Grinder, were on a routine patrol when Ju-88s intercepted their B-24 on August 18. The lead enemy plane conducted a head-on run, accurate 20mm cannon fire knocking out the No. 1 and 2 engines and tearing away the left rudder

Above left: The Junkers Ju-88, such as this one, was encountered by the 479th Antisubmarine Group while operating out of England. (Author's collection)

Above right: The German Fulke-Wolf Fw-200 was a four-engine reconnaissance and bomber used extensively as an anti-shipping platform. (Author's collection)

surface. After the leader's blistering attack, the other Ju-88s joined in for the kill. The planes alternated the attacks as the B-24 began losing altitude as rudder controls became unresponsive; Grider ordered the crew to prepare for ditching.

Only the tail turret gunner heard the order to ditch. He immediately left the turret and approached the waist section, shouting out to the waist and tunnel gunners that ditching was immediate as he passed them. Putting a life raft against the radar turret, he sat down with his back to the raft and awaited the impact. He continued shouting at the waist gunners to take their stations, who were still firing away at the fighters. They did not hear the turret gunner's directions and seemed unhappy to see the tail gunner leave his turret.

The engineer climbed down from his top turret into the pilot's section. As he came forward, he noticed the bombardier leaning over the radar table with his head resting on his arm. Besides the radar position was a jagged four-inch hole from an exploding 20mm shell. The bombardier was dead. The engineer then opened the top hatch and standing, leaned against the armor plate and grabbed the life raft release handle.

Meanwhile, the pilot and co-pilot fought to keep control as the plane approached stall speed. Grinder ordered Moore, "Let her go in." The aircraft's tail dragged along the water; there was no distinguishable bounce or second impact. The nose dropped immediately, and a wall of water swept over the nose, cockpit, and bomb bay. Grinder was knocked unconscious as Lt. Moore reached down to release his safety harness. Hands above his head, he groped, felt jagged edges where the fuselage broke apart, and clambered upwards. After long seconds of pawing at the water, he broke to the surface, gulped in air, and released the cartridge to his life vest.

The engineer, above the flight deck, saw a patch of light and swam upwards. The radio operator did not know what had happened and found himself on the surface. The water filled the waist section from floor to ceiling in the rear. Two in the rear also found themselves on the surface and had no clue how they got there. Two other men were hurled against the bomb bay bulkhead and were either knocked unconscious or killed while the navigator and bombardier were perhaps mortally wounded by cannon fire. After regaining consciousness, Grinder struggled to unfasten his seat belt while swallowing seawater. He managed to unfasten it and finally reached the surface. All the men inflated their life vests. Above the crash scene, the Ju-88s circled while the remaining six crewmen climbed into two dinghies. The survivors took stock of their situation. Three men were relatively unhurt except for bruises and scrapes. Grinder had a swollen black eye and deep scalp cuts, while another was in severe pain and seemed irrational. All of them were dazed and tired; most vomited and were cold. The rafts overturned the following day, causing the drinking water to be lost; the men climbed back in the rafts and spent several more miserable days and nights at sea before being spotted by a B-24 of the 4th Squadron and rescued by a warship. Encounters with enemy aircraft continued through September when the 479th ceased operations as naval B-24 squadrons arrived.

Lieutenant Grinder of the 479th Antisubmarine Group crew adrift in the sea before their rescue by a naval ship on August 22, 1943. (NARA NND983062)

The last plane of the 479th Antisubmarine Group shot down by enemy aircraft, occurred when six Ju-88s intercepted 1st Lieutenant E.T. Finneburgh of the 4th Squadron on September 8. The enemy planes attacked singly, shooting out an engine and shooting the top half of the top turret; the trim tabs and large holes appeared near the gas tanks. One cannon shell exploded inside the cockpit, injuring the pilot. Severe damage forced Finneburgh to ditch the plane, which broke in two when it hit the water. Three of the crew did not survive. The last enemy encounter for the group occurred on October 17, when Capt. J.A. Estes's plane was jumped by 12 Ju-88s, causing damage to the B-24's No. 4 engine right wing. The Liberator managed to evade the enemy and returned to base.

Over the Bay of Biscay, engaging enemy aircraft by the 480th Antisubmarine Group in the Moroccan Sea Frontier proved more severe than a U-boat's defensive firepower. Still, opposition became more severe as the effectiveness of Coastal Command antisubmarine patrols increased. In the Moroccan Sea Frontier, it was not the relatively short-range Ju-88 that opposed aircraft of the 480th Group but the long-range Fw-200, which in many ways was comparable to the B-24. The first encounter of this nature occurred in the last half of July during the 480th Group's antisubmarine blitz, which may have goaded the Germans into action. By August, Fw-200s appeared armed with rapid-firing 20mm cannon, which gave them marked superiority over the B-24's 50-caliber machine guns. The primary mission of the Fw-200s was anti-shipping strikes in which they had a 700-mile range. From this point forward, crews found missions more hazardous, and casualties increased rapidly, with three B-24s lost to enemy aircraft. Air engagements with the Fw-200 proved to be the most dramatic.

Above left: An Fw-200 shortly before being shot down by A B-24 of the 480th Antisubmarine Group. (AFHRA Reel B0522, 1049)

Above right: A B-24D of the 480th Antisubmarine Group shot down the second and last Fw-200 over the Mediterranean. (AFHRA Reel B0638, 338)

Left: Major Mosier shot down this Fw-200 on July 31, 1943. This plane was one of two destroyed by the 480th Antisubmarine Group. (AFHRA Reel B0638, 510)

Fw-200s attacked Convoy MKF-18 on July the 18 and 19 and KMS/OS-52 on July 26 and 27. Air Officer Commanding Gibraltar urgently requested American B-24s to supply coverage for Convoy SL-133. An intense meeting between an Army B-24 from the group and a German Fw-200 followed on the 28th when 1st Lieutenant E.W. Hyde and crew flew convoy coverage. Coverage was routine until a German Fw-200 appeared, attempting to sink one of the convoy's stragglers 15 miles behind the main body. Hyde immediately headed towards the beleaguered ship, and the two planes exchanged heavy gunfire at close range. The German gunners were accurate, scoring hits on all four of the Liberator's engines and killing the top turret gunner, Sergeant J.G. Kehoe. Hyde's gunners meanwhile scored mortal hits on the enemy plane, causing it to cartwheel into the water.

A second Fw-200 to lose an aerial engagement occurred when a Liberator piloted by Captain Gerald L. Mosier caught the enemy plane by surprise on July 31, sending it into the sea.

On August 17, a B-24D piloted by Captain Hugh D. Maxwell Jr was on convoy coverage 300 miles west of Lisbon when two Fw-200s were spotted on radar and visually seen at a distance of one mile, beginning to conduct a bombing run against the convoy. The nearest Fw fired a burst toward the approaching Liberator. Captain Maxwell followed behind while the second Fw closed in on the Liberator. The three planes were in line, and all opened fire simultaneously. The first enemy plane dove to 50ft (15m), with the B-24 and the other Fw-200 following. The Fw behind the B-24 opened with its front and rear 20mm cannons, damaging the Liberator's No. 3 and 4 engines, and large holes appeared in one of the wings. Captain Maxwell continued to intercept the first Fw, scoring hits on the lead aircraft; it burst into flames and fell into the sea. The tail, right waist, and top turret gunner returned fire on the rear enemy aircraft. Still, the Liberator was nearly out of control, and the crew took up their ditching stations.

The B-24's right wing struck the water; the plane skidded and made a 180-degree turn before breaking apart into three pieces. The pilot and co-pilot escaped through the broken windshield, the navigator and bombardier through the escape hatch, and two others escaped through a break in the fuselage near the waist windows. At the same time, the tail gunner went through the top of the turret, which had partially broken off. Seven survivors out of the ten on board survived and climbed into dinghies, all suffering from shrapnel wounds. One of the escort vessels picked them up along with survivors from the first Fw-200. Eyewitnesses aboard the vessel claimed to have seen the German plane crash into the water.

Engagements with enemy aircraft by the 480th Antisubmarine Group continued sporadically through September and October, with the last occurring on October 7. The last Liberator loss to enemy aircraft occurred on September 18 when Captain Lawrence E. Jarnagin reported he was engaging an enemy plane; there were no further communications. The 480th Antisubmarine began encountering fewer German aircraft as the Allies secured Sicily [Operation *Husky*] on August 17, 1943, thus effectively removing the threat. At the same time, the 479th and later Navy B-24 squadrons experienced far more enemy aircraft due to operating over the English Channel and the Bay of Biscay. The two groups encountered 220

A German Fw-200 shot down Captain Hugh Maxwell, shown here, and his crew on **August 17, 1943.** (AFHRA Reel B0638, 724)

enemy aircraft, with the 479th encountering 165 enemy aircraft compared to the 480 Group's 55. Still, the latter shot down eight planes while its sister group in England destroyed three. However, the 479th encountered the far deadlier Ju-88. Interceptions by German aircraft continued throughout August and October for the 480th Group, with one B-24D lost to an enemy aircraft on September 18, when Captain Jarnagin and his crew disappeared.

Enemy Aircraft Encounters

	479th A/S Group	480th A/S Group	Total
Aircraft Encountered	165	55	220
Destroyed	3	8	11
Probably Destroyed	1	1	2
Damaged	4	6	10
Probably Damaged	8	0	8
Total Destroyed or Damaged	16 (a)	15 (b)	31

(a) All Ju-88s
(b) Destroyed: 5 Fw-200s, 2 Do-24's, 1 Do-26, 1 Ju-88 probably destroyed, 2 Fw-200s damaged, 4 Ju-88's damaged.

Source: *The Antisubmarine Command, U.S. Air Force Historical Study No.107*, Prepared by the Assistance Chief of Staff, Intelligence Historical Division, pp442 and 447. For additional information see pp433–455.

B-24s damaged or destroyed by enemy aircraft

	479 A/S Group	480th A/S Group	Total
Destroyed	3	4	7
Damaged	7	6	13
Total	10	10	20

Source: *The Antisubmarine Command, U.S. Air Force Historical Study No. 107*, Prepared by the Assistant Chief of Staff, Intelligence Historical Division, pp 442, 447.

A German Dornier Do-26 flying boat under attack by Capt. McKeon and crew of the 480th Antisubmarine Group on September 10, 1943. (AFHRA Reel A0522, 496)

Above: Captain McKeon and his crew shot down this German Do-24 flying boat on September 10, 1943. (NFHRA Reel 0B638, 338)

Right: Major L.E. Jarnagin (then Captain), commanding officer of the 2nd Antisubmarine Squadron at an award ceremony. He and his crew went missing in action while encountering an enemy plane on September 18, 1943. (AFHRA Reel B0638, 380)

Chapter 8
Conclusion

The history of USAAF antisubmarine operations is a story of how an essential aspect of ASW grew out of necessity with confusing jurisdiction between the Army and Navy. There were no official plans to meet the U-boat threat at the beginning. The I Bomber Command assumed responsibility for creating an AAF organization to conduct such a task, which the Navy closely guarded as a defensive means to protect convoys. There was no unity of command as each service jockeyed into position to claim its authority. The Army threw planes and unskilled crews into the U-boat war since the Navy had limited resources.

The birth of USAAF antisubmarine operations grew out of necessity with confused jurisdiction about which branch, the Army or Navy, should take on the battle against the U-boat. It was born when German submarines operated with near impunity during the first year of the United States' entry into the war. The Antisubmarine Command replaced I Bomber Command to consolidate and streamline the resources available at the time and, in doing so, attempted to create an independent force separate from the oversight of the Navy. Meanwhile, the Navy undertook a defensive doctrine that would protect convoys sailing off the Eastern Seaboard. At the same time, the AAF pursued an offensive strategy to meet U-boats hundreds of miles off the coast. Army authorities argued it had the means to conduct such warfare.

AAF groups, wings, and individual squadrons met the challenge and contributed to antisubmarine operations with Army authorities arguing it had the means to conduct such warfare, which wasn't entirely true in 1942. AAF groups, wings, and individual squadrons met the challenge, although the numbers do not reflect it. It is quite possible that AAF antisubmarine operations, independent from the Navy, may have contributed significantly to the effort if they had begun operations months earlier. As it was, most of the strength during 1942 remained tied to the Navy's defensive strategy. By the time of dissolution, the antisubmarine command was nearing a level of experience and had the proper aircraft fitted with radar. Therefore, eliminating the Army's antisubmarine command may have been premature. The potentialities of the Army's antisubmarine operations, if given the opportunity beyond September 1943 and allowed to operate from the UK, will never be known as General Arnold allowed the Navy to undertake the task. At the same time, the danger of U-boats remained high, especially in the Bay of Biscay. By September 1943, squadrons of Navy B-24s began arriving in England to take over the mission. Still, it would take months before such units would be effective, in which Army squadrons could have been operational and continued with the battle. By the end of August 1943, the AAF still possessed a significant number of ASW aircraft and trained personnel in its inventory compared to the Navy; the latter would assume the mission in the late summer of 1943.

The record of the Army's antisubmarine mission is mixed at best. Except for the 479th and 480th Antisubmarine Groups, it's a story about a great deal of effort bringing minimal results, as it took until 1943 to train personnel and equip them with VLR aircraft to engage the enemy successfully. Both groups displayed that an effective fighting force could be trained and equipped with radar-equipped B-24 Liberators. That was the goal of the AAF: to create a specialized and mobile task force capable of engaging in an offensive war. Therefore, eliminating the Army's antisubmarine command may have been premature. If given the opportunity beyond September 1943 and allowed to operate from the UK, the potentialities of the Army's antisubmarine operations may have contributed significantly.

Appendix A
U-boats Sunk by AAF Antisubmarine Squadrons

Date	Squadron	U-boat
July 6, 1942	59th BS	U-153
July 7, 1942	396 BS	U-701
August 22, 1942	45th BS	U-654
October 2, 1942	99th BS	U-512
March 22, 1943	2nd	U-524
July 7, 1943	1st	U-951
July 9, 1943	1st	U-435
July 12, 1943	1st	U-506
July 20, 1943	19th/58 Squadron/RAF	U-558
July 28, 1943	4th/224 Squadron/RAF	U-404
August 2, 1943	4th/415 Squadron/RCAF	U-706
Claimed as Sunk		
		U-519
		U-232
Known to be Damaged		
		U-183
		U-211
		U-752

Source: Compiled by the author.

The table below shows that the Navy Air Force took the ASW role in the Eastern Sea Frontier, Guantanamo Sector, Puerto Rico, Trinidad, and Bermuda. However, it still lacked adequate VLR aircraft in many operational areas.

Order of Battle Antisubmarine Aircraft (August 1943)

Location	Type and Number of Aircraft			
	VLR	LR	MR	SR
Iceland				
USN	0	10	0	0
AAF	14	0	19	0
Greenland				
USN	0	0	8	0
AAF	0	6	0	0
Newfoundland and Nova Scotia				
USN	7	0	0	0
AAF	12	0	0	0
Eastern Sea Frontier				
USN	0	17	20	158
AAF	20	0	34	0
Gulf Sea Frontier				
USN	19	0	15	0
AAF	20	0	34	0
Panama Sea Frontier				
USN	0	11	0	32
Guantanamo Sector				
USN	0	33	0	14
Puerto Rico Sector				
USN	0	1	8	28
AAF	0	0	6	0
Trinidad Sector				
USN	0	24	4	14
AAF	5	0	21	6
Curacao-Aruba Sector				
USN	0	4	0	14
AAF	4	0	6	25
Bermuda				
USN	10	8	0	15
Moroccan Sector				
AAF and RAF	24	33	55	0
United Kingdom				
USN	0	15	0	0
AAF	45	139	173	0

VLR (Very Long Range), LR (Long Range), MR (Medium Range), SR (Short Range)

Source: Air Force Historical Research Agency (AFHRA) staff at Maxwell AFB, Alabama Reel 523, 485-486.

Appendix B
Lineage of USAAF Antisubmarine Squadrons

Antisubmarine Squadron	Previous Bombardment Squadron Designation
1st	361st
2nd	523rd
3rd	29th
4th	40th
5th	41st
6th	393rd
7th	78th
8th	79th
9th	80th
10th	92nd
11th	516th
12th	517th
13th	518th
14th	519th
15th	520th
16th	521st
17th	522nd
18th	362nd
19th	363rd
20th	421st
21st	128th (Observation Squadron)
22nd	46th
23rd	76th
24th	843rd
25th	

Source: *Air Force Combat Units of World War Two*. Washington DC. Government Printing Office, 1961 and compiled by the author.

Appendix C
Squadron Information (July 1943)

Squadron/Group	Type and Number of Aircraft	Location
1st and 2nd	24/B-24s	Port Lyautey, Africa
2nd and 4th	57/B-24s	St. Eval, England
3rd	13 B-24s	Ft. Dix, New Jersey
	4 B-25s	
5th	11 B-24s	Westover Field, Mass
	6 B-25s	
6th	8 B-24s	Westover Field, Mass
7th	none	Jacksonville, Fla
8th	12/B-24s	
9th	9 B-24s	Miami, Fla
10th	15 B-24s	Galveston, Texas
	1 B-25s	
11th	10 B-24s	Ft. Dix, New Jersey
	4 B-25s	
	1 B-25	
	3 B-34s	
12th	5 B-24s	Langley Field, Virginia
	8 B-25s	
13th	8 B-24s	Granier, N.H.
	9 B-25s	
14th	6 B-24s	Otis Field, Mass
	8	
15th	11 B-24s	Batista Field, Cuba
	9 B-25s	
	2 B-34s	
16th	7 B-25s	Charleston, S.C.
	1 B-34	
17th	1 B-24	Miami, Florida
18th	33 B-24s	Langley Field, Virginia
20th	15 B-17s	Mitchell Field, New York
	1 B-24	
21st	6 B-25s	Gulfport, Miss
23rd	16 B-25s	Drew Field, Fla.
24th	11 B-25s	Westover Field, Mass
25th	12 B-25s	Jacksonville, Fla

Source: Air Force Historical Research Agency (AFHRA) staff at Maxwell AFB, Alabama Reel 522, 465–471.

Appendix D
Bombardment Groups Assigned to Antisubmarine Command (July 1943)

Group	Squadrons
2nd	20th
	49th
	96th
	45th
13th (Heavy)	39th
	40th
	41st
	293rd
40th (Medium)	25th
	29th
	44th
	45th
	74th
	395th
45th (Medium)	78th
	79th
	80th
	78th
377th (Heavy)	516th
	517th
	518th
	519th
378 (Heavy)	520th
	521st
	522nd
	523rd

Source: *Air Force Combat Units of World War Two*. Washington DC. Government Printing Office, 1961.

Selected Bibliography

Carey, Alan C, *Galloping Ghosts of the Brazilian Coast*, Lincoln, Nebraska: iUniverse, 2004
Carey, Alan C, *Sighted Sub, Sank Same, Havertown*, Pennsylvania: Casemate, 2019
Blair, Clay, *Hitler's U-boat War*, Modern Library, New York, 2000
Goss, Chris, *Bloody Biscay: The History of V Gruppe/Kampfgeschwader 40*, Crecy Publishing, 2001
Kelshall, Gaylord T.M., *The U-boat in the Caribbean*, Annapolis, Maryland. United States Naval, Institute, 1994
Niestle, Axel, *German U-boat Losses During World War One*, Frontline Books, 2014

Government Documents

U.S. Radar Operational Characteristics of Radar, Joint Committee on New Weapons and Equipment Classified by Tactical Application, U.S. Radar Operational Characteristics of Radar Classified by Tactical Application, FTP-217, 72
Schoenfeld, *Stalking the U-boat: USAAF Offensive Antisubmarine Operations in World War Two*, Smithsonian History of Aviation Series. Washington and London. Smithsonian Institution Press. 1995
Sternhell and Alan M. Thorndike, OEG Report No. 51, *Antisubmarine Warfare in World War Two*, Operations Evaluation Group, Office of the Chief of Naval Operations, Navy Department, Washington D.C., 1946
Warnock, A. Timothy, *Air Power Versus U-boats, Confronting Hitler's Submarine Menace in the European Theater*, Air Force History and Museum Programs, 1999
Warnock, Timothy, *The Battle Against the U-boat in the American Theater*, The Air Force History Support Office
Air Force Combat Squadrons of World War Two, Washington DC. Government Printing Office, 1961
Air Force Combat Squadrons of World War Two, Washington D.C., Government Printing Office
*The Army Air Forces in World War Two, Vol 1, Plans and Early Opera*tions (January 1939 to August 1942, edited by Wesley Frank Craven and James Lea Cate. Office of Air Force History, Washington D.C., 1983
The Army Air Forces in World War Two, Vol 2, Europe: Torch to Pointblank (August 1942 to December 1943), Office of Air Force History, Washington D.C., 1983
The Battle Against the U-boat in the American Theater, Albert F. Simpson Historical Research Center, Office of the Air Force History Headquarters, USAF, 1982
The Antisubmarine Command, U.S. Air Force Historical Study No. 107 (Short Title-AAFRH-7), Prepared by the Assistant Chief of Staff, Intelligence Historical Division
U.S. Air Force Research Agency, Maxwell Air Force Base, Alabama Reels A0522
U.S. Air Force Research Agency A0523
U.S. Air Force Research Agency A0635
U.S. Air Force Research Agency A4058
U.S. Air Force Research Agency A4088
U.S. Air Force Research Agency A4067
U.S. Air Force Research Agency A4073

U.S. Air Force Research Agency A4070
U.S. Air Force Research Agency, B0635
U.S. Air Force Research Agency B0637
U.S. Air Force Research Agency C0174

Websites
U-boat Archive, U-boat Archive–Index of ASW Incidents (uboatarchive.net)
U-Boat Net, The U-boat Wars 1939–45 (Kriegsmarine) and 1914–18 (Kaiserliche Marine) and Allied Warships of WWII–uboat.net

Endnotes

Chapter 1
1. Carey, Alan C. Sighted Sub, Sank Same, Havertown, Pennsylvania: Casemate Publishing (2019), 11.
2. Carey, Alan C. Sighted Sub, Sank Same, xv.

Chapter 2
1. The Antisubmarine Command, U.S. Air Force Historical Study No. 107, 5.
2. Air Force Historical Research Agency (AFHRA) staff at Maxwell AFB, Alabama Reel A4058, 126-127.
3. The Antisubmarine Command, U.S. Air Force Historical Study No. 107 (Short Title-AAFRH-7) Prepared by the Assistant Chief of Staff, Intelligence Historical Division., 238.
4. The Antisubmarine Command, U.S. Air Force Historical Study No. 107, 20.
5. Air Force Historical Research Agency (AFHRA), Reel A4058, 482.
6. The Antisubmarine Command, U.S. Air Force Historical Study No. 107, 25.
7. Air Force Historical Research Agency (AFHRA), Reel A4058, 482.
8. The Antisubmarine Command, U.S. Air Force Historical Study No. 107, 31.
9. Air Force Historical Research Agency (AFHRA), Reel A4058, 129.
10. The Antisubmarine Command, U.S. Air Force Historical Study No. 107, 38.
11. Air Force Historical Research Agency (AFHRA), Reel A4058, 447.

Chapter 3
1. The Antisubmarine Command, U.S. Air Force Historical Study No. 107 (Short Title-AAFRH-7) Prepared by the Assistant Chief of Staff, Intelligence Historical Division., 46-47.
2. Air Force Historical Research Agency, Reel A4058, 115-116.
3. (AFHRA) staff at Maxwell AFB, Alabama, Reel 523, 79.
4. The Air Force Historical Agency, 79.
5. The Antisubmarine Command, U.S. Air Force Historical Study No. 107, 57-58.
6. Air Force Historical Research Agency, Reel 522, 79.
7. Air Force Historical Research Agency (AFHRA) staff at Maxwell AFB, Alabama, Reel 523, 407.

Chapter 4
1. Carey, Alan C. Sighted Sub, Sank Same, Havertown, Pennsylvania (2019), 37.
2. Carey, Alan C. Sighted Sub, 38.
3. U-boat Archive - U-512 - Interrogation of P/W Machon by Lt. Gherardi (uboatarchive.net)

Chapter 5
1. Sir John Slessor "bloodied themselves," Air Force Historical Research Agency (AFHRA) staff at Maxwell AFB, Alabama, Reel 4058, 489.
2. Air Force Historical Research Agency (AFHRA) staff at Maxwell AFB, Alabama, Reel A4058, 319.
3. Air Force Historical Research Agency (AFHRA), Reel A4058, 329.
4. Air Force Historical Research Agency (AFHRA), Reel A4058, 355.

5. Air Force Historical Research Agency (AFHRA), Reel A4058, 359.
6. Air Force Historical Research Agency (AFHRA), Reel A4070, 616.
7. Air Force Historical Research Agency (AFHRA), Reel A4070, 874.

Chapter 7

1. The Antisubmarine Command, U.S. Air Force Historical Study No. 107 (Short Title-AAFRH-7). Prepared by the Assistant Chief of Staff, Intelligence Historical Division,191.

Index

I Bomber Command
13th Bombardment Squadron,
18th Antisubmarine Squadron
18th Reconnaissance Squadron,
19th Antisubmarine Squadron
1st Reconnaissance Squadron
20th Bombardment Squadron
22nd Bombardment Group
25th Antisubmarine Wing
26th Antisubmarine Group
1st Antisubmarine Squadron
2nd Antisubmarine Squadron
34th Bombardment Group
40th Bombardment Group
40th Bombardment Squadron
43rd Bombardment Group
45th Bombardment Group
479th Antisubmarine Group
480th Antisubmarine Group
59th Bombing Squadron
1st Antisubmarine Squadron
6th Antisubmarine Squadron
8th Antisubmarine Squadron
99th Bombardment Squadron
A-20
A-29
Alexander, A.V.
AN/APS
Andrews, Adolphus
Army Air Force Antisubmarine Command (AAFASC)
Arnold Henry "Hap"
Assistant Chief of Staff, Operations Division (OPD)
ASW
ASWORG
B-17
B-18
B-24
B-25

BdU
Bowles, Edward
Broussard, George
Caribbean Sea Frontier (CARIBSEAFRON)
CINCLANT
Clausen, Nicolai
Coastal Command
COMINCH
Commander, Naval Authorities in North African waters (COMNAVNAW)
Degan, Horst
Dönitz, Karl
Eastern Sea Frontier
Eighth Bomber Command
First Antisubmarine Group (Provisional)
Fleet Air Wing Fifteen (FAW 15
FW-200
Gallmeier, Charles
Geir
Gondola
Groover, M.E.
Gulf Sea Frontier
Hamilton, Joseph
Hammer, Arthur
Harden, James
Hartenstein, Werner
Jarnagin, Lawrence
Ju-88
Kane, Harry
King, Ernest J.
Larson, Westside
Low, Francis S., 42
Marshal, George C.
Maxwell Jr, Hugh
McNarney, Joesph
Moore, Howard
New Ground
Noble, Percy
North Atlantic Naval Coastal Frontier (NANCF)
Operation Drumbeat

Operational Training Squadron
Panama Sea Frontier
PB4Y
Port Lyautey
Roberts, Jack
SADU
Salam, Ernst
Sanford, William
Schultze, Wolfgang
SCR-517
Slessor, John
Tenth Fleet
Tidewater Tilli
Tuttle, Arthur
U.S. 10th Fleet
U-109
U-123
U-125
U-129
U-130
U-153
U-158
U-232
U-404
U-435
U-503
U-512
U-519
U-524
U-558
U-654
U-66
U-701
U-706
U-951
Würdemann, Erich

Other books you might like:

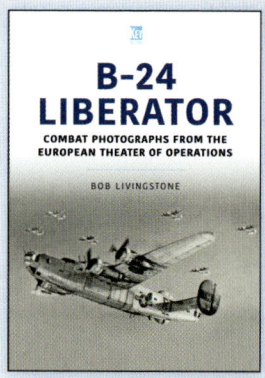
Historic Military Aircraft Series, Vol. 21

Historic Military Aircraft Series, Vol. 20

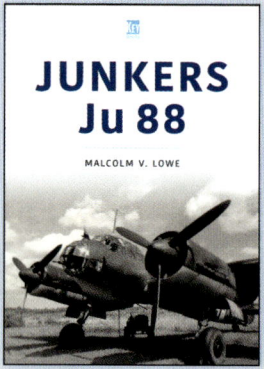
Military Aircraft Series, Vol. 15

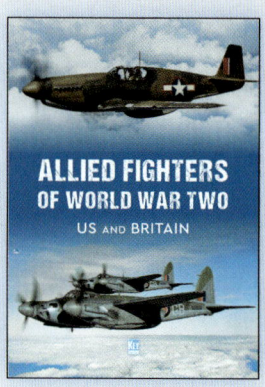

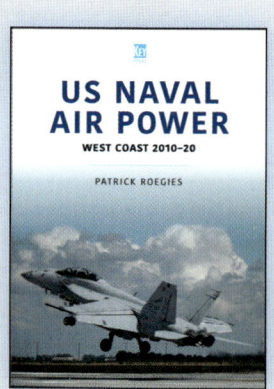
Air Forces Series, Vol. 2

For our full range of titles please visit:
shop.keypublishing.com/books

VIP Book Club

Sign up today and receive
TWO FREE E-BOOKS

Be the first to find out about our forthcoming book releases and receive exclusive offers.

Register now at **keypublishing.com/vip-book-club**

Our VIP Book Club is a 100% spam-free zone, and we will never share your email with anyone else. You can read our full privacy policy at: privacy.keypublishing.com